Leverage for Good

Leverage for Good

An Introduction to the
New Frontiers of Philanthropy
and Social Investment

Lester M. Salamon

OXFORD
UNIVERSITY PRESS

OXFORD
UNIVERSITY PRESS

Oxford University Press is a department of the University of Oxford.
It furthers the University's objective of excellence in research, scholarship,
and education by publishing worldwide.

Oxford   New York
Auckland   Cape Town   Dar es Salaam   Hong Kong   Karachi
Kuala Lumpur   Madrid   Melbourne   Mexico City   Nairobi
New Delhi   Shanghai   Taipei   Toronto

With offices in
Argentina   Austria   Brazil   Chile   Czech Republic   France   Greece
Guatemala   Hungary   Italy   Japan   Poland   Portugal   Singapore
South Korea   Switzerland   Thailand   Turkey   Ukraine   Vietnam

Oxford is a registered trademark of Oxford University Press
in the UK and certain other countries.

Published in the United States of America by
Oxford University Press
198 Madison Avenue, New York, NY 10016

Library of Congress Cataloging-in-Publication Data

Salamon, Lester M.
Leverage for good : an introduction to the new frontiers of philanthropy and social investment / Lester M. Salamon.
pages cm
Includes bibliographical references.
ISBN 978-0-19-937652-0 (hardback : alk. paper)—ISBN 978-0-19-937653-7 (pbk. : alk. paper)
1. Endowments.   2. Charities.   3. Social service.   I. Title.
HV16.S26 2014
361.7—dc23
2013040023

9 8 7 6 5 4 3 2 1
Printed in the United States of America
on acid-free paper

"There are moments in history when the needs of an age prompt lasting, promising innovation."

—Monitor Institute, 2009

Contents

List of Figures

List of Tables

List of Boxes

Foreword

Rip Rapson

American philanthropy is in the midst of one of its most turbulent and interesting transformations in nearly a century. The changing terrain of charitable giving is evinced by an at-times baffling proliferation of new actors, new tools, and new organizations, challenging everything from philanthropy's traditional ways of doing business to how we think about defining our social objectives. Navigating that terrain is difficult enough for someone whose organization is in the thick of it, let alone for newcomers to the field.

That reality makes the present monograph, and the companion volume for which it serves as an introduction, indispensable reference points for new and experienced practitioners alike. They provide what the sector has long been missing: a coherent, comprehensive, and compelling road map that brings together an array of disparate pieces into a coherent whole. They will provide a resource and shortcut that will not only help my organization—the Kresge Foundation—but also, I believe, the sector as a whole emerge from these transformations more organizationally effective, vibrant, and vital. That is why we at Kresge so enthusiastically supported the creation of these volumes, and why we are so pleased with the results.

Indeed, I wish this material had existed five years ago when Kresge began its own transformation—a transformation that is emblematic of, and aligns with so many of, the trends and themes outlined in the pages that follow. So allow me to start by describing the particulars of Kresge's experience, in the hope that they will help illustrate the importance of this project for the sector as a whole.

The Kresge Foundation's Path

The Kresge Foundation I joined in 2006 was defined by one tool—the capital challenge grant, which sought to build the capacity of nonprofits by helping them complete capital campaigns for building projects. Kresge's brand was crystal clear: we were synonymous with bricks and mortar.

It was a remarkable legacy, one we are proud of to this day. Not only had we assisted thousands of organizations in getting important projects to the finish line, we had also defined an admirable set of competencies that distinguished us within the philanthropic cosmos:

- We got good at something and stuck to our knitting—as such, we were able to separate the good project from the great project and readily identify the strengths and weaknesses of proposals.

- Grant seekers were very clear about what we funded—organizations had to go through rigorous analysis, but didn't have to bend themselves into pretzels trying to guess at our expectations.

- And we provided critical leverage—our funding served as a catalyst to bring others to the table.

But it was clear to me—and to the Kresge board—that the time had come for a refresh. From our perspective, what was needed was not necessarily more new buildings, but a more expansive way of thinking about society's most intractable problems. And yet we wanted to carry forward those qualities that had served us well: sophisticated insight into good ideas, clarity of purpose, and high leverage.

We began reconstructing the foundation topically, assessing field by field how we might expand opportunities in America's cities. We would do that by investing in the revitalization of Detroit, attacking health disparities, mitigating and adapting to climate change, increasing the resilience of human service organizations, improving postsecondary access and success among low-income and nontraditional students, and elevating the importance of arts and culture in community identity and revitalization.

Because this new constellation of challenges didn't respond to just one "tool," we also had to recalibrate how we worked.

This has all taken a while to settle out. We now have sharply etched subject matter strategies. We've built program teams that convene and invest in research, networks, advocacy, and communications strategies. We've stretched our capital support spectrum to include a variety of philanthropic instruments. We've created a social investments practice that over the next five years will deploy $150 million in loans, guarantees, linked deposits, and direct investments. And we've tested the edges of risk and the complexities of working across sectors.

A Recalibrated Orientation to Capital

What we haven't yet fully done, however, is to leave the safe and familiar moorings of approaching most funding opportunities with a grant-centric perspective.

Like many foundations, Kresge has deeply coded in its DNA a two-step analysis that defines how we spend our money:

- First, does a proposal from a nonprofit fit our strategy?

- And second, should we make a grant to support that organization?

At a first level of analysis, there is absolutely nothing wrong with this formulation. It calls for a strategic intentionality that is entirely appropriate. Indeed, the first part of the question is essential—we start by asking what problem we're trying to solve.

The nuance comes with the second part of the question. Given the diversity of problems we're seeking to crack, it seems odd to assume that the right tool for the job will always be a grant to an organization. In fact, it is virtually never the case that a stand-alone grant solves the entirety of a problem or allows us to scale impact. And in fairness to grantees, they rarely claim otherwise.

We've accordingly sought to ask a different question: what is the set of tools or approaches that are most likely to move the needle on the problem we seek to address?

There may be a grant somewhere in that mix, but there may also be a program-related investment, a prize, or even a social-impact bond. And if there is a grant, it might be for any number of purposes—to support operations, projects, research, public information campaigns, advocacy, policy reform, and many other activities. At the risk of being ridiculously simplistic, we're testing what it means to be problem-solvers first and foremost. That means starting with the problem and then, and only then, selecting the form of capital—whether financial, intellectual, or reputational—most suited to fixing it.

The financial crisis of 2008 launched that approach. Our social investment practice's very first investments were driven by the problem at hand. Human service organizations providing food, shelter, and other emergency services needed a bridge—to an improved climate for donations, to the receipt of government payables, to an easing of personal economic crisis among their clients. We made 14 zero-interest, three-year loans to those organizations. They were a stopgap and they weren't innovative, but they were what the organizations needed. And they started us on a new way of doing business. We have since navigated from that starting point to a far more sophisticated and complex portfolio that has vastly expanded our capacity and effectiveness as a philanthropic organization. It has made us more rigorous about starting with a problem, rather than with a tool.

The Woodward Corridor Real Estate Initiative in our hometown of Detroit is an example. In mid-2012, a senior program officer on our Detroit team sent out an e-mail pointing to the incredible diversity of some two-dozen emerging real estate projects along the Woodward Avenue corridor. These projects needed to come to fruition, he argued, if we were to achieve our goals of introducing density, diversity, vibrancy, and walkability to Detroit's core. He suggested that we needed a "capital war chest" that would provide the critical missing pieces of financing. We responded by creating a "hybrid fund structure" that will allow us to use the capacity of a strong intermediary (for lending purposes) while maintaining control of our most flexible capital tools (grants and guarantees) for strategic deployment alongside and/or in support of our externally managed debt capital.

Three Challenges

But these approaches are still the exception at Kresge. Three obstacles have made the pivot toward a more creative use of capital difficult, obstacles that face many philanthropic institutions.

First is the capacity to work across sectors, with a particular eye toward finance.

Investing in social change implicates a larger context occupied by public and private partners. That requires that we understand how philanthropic capital fits: how it will combine with the actions of others to help lever changes in markets, behaviors, and policy. Each sector will ask different things of the foundation, but each will almost certainly contribute in some measure to the problems we seek to influence. That, in turn, necessitates that we become conversant in the language and needs of private and public finance, policy, decision-making, and accountability systems—and accordingly rethink our professional development strategies to find a balance between topical expertise and financial dexterity—in short, it necessitates that we become what Lester Salamon in this volume calls a "philanthropic bank."

Second is the ability to break down internal barriers among different program areas within a foundation and work as an integrated whole.

It is the norm rather than the exception that a strategy centered in one topical area will be linked with strategies in other disciplines. In New Orleans, for example, our Environment Team's investments in organizations working for the restoration of the Gulf Coast play off of our Community Development Team's investments in community engagement strategies in the Ninth Ward.

For that reason, social investment practices in foundations will fall short if they are seen simply as a service desk for program teams. Just as program teams need to be more deeply conversant in finance, the social investments function has to more deeply understand programs—they can't be finance jockeys for whom the imperative becomes making a compelling deal, rather than reinforcing program strategy by tackling the biggest social problems in the most effective ways.

Third is bridging the normal divide between the program staff and the investments office.

Our initial gesture at Kresge has been to create a more sustained feedback loop between our investment teams and program teams, under the theory that even having both sides of our house know what the other is up to will make a difference. We've also taken some baby steps toward mission-related investing—trying to identify among all our resources and knowledge those assets that can contribute most readily and directly to our mission. What we do with that information remains an open debate within our staff and among our trustees. But having that information allows us to ground our future path in data, and make some informed choices accordingly.

Concluding Thoughts

Kresge's efforts in pushing ourselves into the social investing arena and organizing around a new way of working are not models—they have simply been our reality. And that reality has at times been a slow, tough, and exasperating slog. That, at core, is what makes the present monograph, and the companion volume it so effectively introduces, so valuable and worth supporting: it won't solve all of these challenges, but it outlines them exhaustively and provides an invaluable overview of the enormous opportunities opening up to bring new resources and new talents to the solution of some of our most intractable problems.

It has been an honor for us at Kresge to support this project, but in truth it wasn't purely a selfless gesture. It will help us, as we believe it will help our partners, our peers, and the sector as a whole, make a more profound and lasting impact on the issues about which we are most passionate. I look forward to returning to it time and again.

Acknowledgments

It has been said that "it takes a village to raise a child." But, as any author knows, the same applies to raising a book. And that is certainly the case here. My debts in bringing this book, and the larger companion volume on which it heavily leans, to fruition have been enormous, and I gratefully acknowledge them here. They are owed to Rip Rapson, President of the Kresge Foundation, who early on recognized the niche that this book and its companion would fill and helped provide the support and encouragement that made them possible; to William Burckart, who assisted me in organizing the project, recruiting authors, maintaining contact, and managing the substantial paper flow that any project of this scope entails; to Luther Ragin, now at the Global Impact Investing Network (GIIN), who encouraged the effort and gave selflessly of his time to review most of the chapters in the companion volume and offer comments and advice; to the members of the Project Advisory Committee (listed in Appendix A) for their enormously helpful comments and assistance at numerous points in the process; to David Erickson and his colleagues at the Federal Reserve Bank of San Francisco for providing meeting space at the Fed and other support and encouragement to our work; to Bill Dietel and Mario Morino, who agreed to write a Preface and Foreword, respectively, for the companion volume, to introduce the work to the broader audiences it seeks to address and who provided inspiration along the way; to the authors of the companion volume (listed in Appendix B), incredibly thoughtful and dedicated professionals all, who spent what I am sure is far more hours than they ever imagined responding to my detailed comments and suggestions to get their chapters into a consistent form and make this complicated topic accessible to the broadest possible audience; to David McBride, the social sciences acquisition editor at Oxford, who skillfully moved this book and its companion through the complex Oxford review process; to Chelsea Newhouse at the Johns Hopkins Center for Civil Studies, who patiently and professionally handled the process of bringing the manuscript into conformance with the protocols and formats that Oxford procedures stipulate; and last, but by no means least, to my lovely wife, Lynda, who put up over an unforgivably long period with the unavoidable distractedness and preoccupation that writing inevitably entails, and did so with enormous understanding and support.

Without taking away anything from the enormous assistance I received from all of these friends and colleagues, at the end of the day I recognize that responsibility for this final product, with whatever faults it might still have, belongs with me, and I accept it fully.

Lester M. Salamon

Annapolis, Maryland

September 21, 2013

Chapter 1

Introduction: The Revolution on the Frontiers of Philanthropy and Social Investment

On September 28, 2011, *Microfinance Africa*, a newsletter serving the microfinance industry on the African continent, reported news of an important, if unusual, development designed to help East Africa cope with the region's food shortage and resulting skyrocketing food prices. An unexpected consortium had come together to channel US$25 million to a series of small and medium-sized East African agricultural enterprises whose businesses could help link the region's small-holder farmers to improved production and marketing opportunities.* Although the US Agency for International Development was a party to this consortium, this was not your normal top-down, government-funded development project. Rather, USAID had teamed up with three foundations (the UK-based Gatsby Charitable Foundation, and the US-based Rockefeller and Gates foundations), a major US investment firm (J.P. Morgan Social Finance), and Pearl Capital Partners, a private, Kampala-based investment company dedicated to channeling private equity to small-holder agricultural enterprises in Africa.[1]

What may be most unusual about this deal in the current climate of development assistance, philanthropy, and finance, however, is that it is no longer unusual at all. Rather, it is an example of what students of the field have begun referring to as "yin-yang" deals, deals that bring together, as in Chinese thought, seemingly contrary forces that turn out to be uniquely capable of producing new life forms when taking advantage of their interdependencies.[2] In the present arrangement, USAID managed to stimulate the investment of $25 million into building a robust agribusiness sector in East Africa with only $1.5 million of its own money, and all of that in the form of technical assistance to small and medium-sized businesses funded out of President Obama's flagship Feed the Future initiative. The investment fund itself was assembled by combining a USAID guarantee of an $8 million loan from J.P. Morgan's Social Finance Unit that was further leveraged by

* Unless otherwise noted, dollar amounts reported are in US dollars.

$17 million in equity investments made by the three foundations, which functioned in this deal as "philanthropic banks" rather than traditional grant-making charities.[3]

A significant revolution appears to be underway on the frontiers of philanthropy and social investment.

Sizable yin-yang deals of this sort are slowly becoming the new normal in efforts to combat the enormous social, economic, and environmental problems that confront our world at the present time. And none too soon. With the resources of both governments and traditional philanthropy barely growing or in decline, yet the problems of poverty, ill-health, and environmental degradation ballooning daily, it is increasingly clear that new models for financing and promoting social and environmental objectives have become urgently needed.

A bewildering array of new instruments and institutions has surfaced [to finance social-purpose activities].

Fortunately, a significant revolution appears to be underway on the frontiers of philanthropy that is providing at least a partial, though still embryonic, response to this dilemma. The heart of this revolution is a massive explosion in the tools of philanthropy and social investment, in the instruments and institutions being deployed to mobilize private resources in support of social and environmental objectives. Where earlier such support was limited to charitable grants and gifts made available directly by individuals or through charitable foundations and corporate giving programs, now a bewildering array of new instruments and institutions has surfaced— loans, loan guarantees, private equity, barter arrangements, social stock exchanges, bonds, secondary markets, investment funds, and many more. Indeed, the world of philanthropy seems to be experiencing a Big Bang similar in kind, if not in exact form, to the one thought to have produced the planets and stars of our solar system.

Figure 1.1
Philanthropy's "Big Bang"

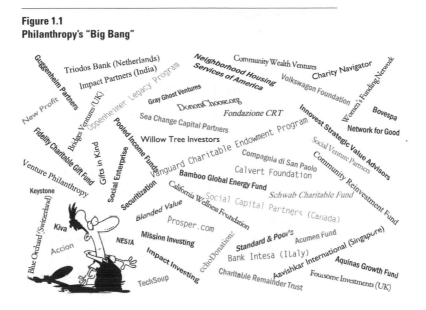

Even a quick glance at the emerging landscape on the frontiers of contemporary philanthropy around the world yields a rich harvest of unfamiliar names and terms: Bovespa in Brazil; Social Capital Partners in Canada; Impact Investment Exchange in Singapore; Acumen Fund, Root Capital, and New Profit in the US; Bridges Ventures, Big Society Capital and NESTA in the UK; Blue Orchard in Switzerland; Aavishkaar International in India; Willow Tree Impact Investors in Dubai; Calvert Foundation; the Schwab Charitable Fund; the Community Reinvestment Fund; community development finance institutions; TechSoup Global; conversion foundations; and many more (see Figure 1.1).

At the core of this enormous proliferation of entities lie four important processes of change. In particular, contemporary philanthropy is moving:

- **Beyond grants**: deploying a variety of new financial tools for promoting social purposes—loans, loan guarantees, equity-type investments, securitization, fixed-income instruments, and, most recently, social-impact bonds.

- **Beyond foundations**: creating a host of new actors as the institutional structures through which social-purpose finance is proceeding—capital aggregators, secondary markets, social stock exchanges, social enterprise brokers, internet portals, to name just a few.

- **Beyond bequests**: forming charitable or social-purpose capital pools not simply through the gifts of wealthy individuals, but also from the privatization of formerly public or quasi-public assets or the establishment of specialized social-purpose investment funds.

- **Beyond cash:** utilizing new barter arrangements and internet capabilities to facilitate the giving not just of money, but of a variety of in-kind forms of assistance, whether it be volunteer time or computer hardware and software.

Leverage is the mechanism that allows limited energy to be translated into greater power.

Behind these movements is a common imperative, usefully summarized in a single word: *leverage.* Leverage is the mechanism that allows limited energy to be translated into greater power. It is what allowed Archimedes to claim that, given a lever and a place to stand, he could "move the whole world."[4] In the philanthropic context it means finding a way to go beyond the limited flow of charitable resources generated by the earnings on foundation assets or the annual contributions of individuals to catalyze for social and environmental purposes some portion of the far more enormous investment assets resident in banks, pension funds, insurance companies, mutual funds, and the accounts of high net worth individuals.[5]

The upshot is the emergence of a "new frontier" of philanthropy and social investing that differs from twentieth-century philanthropy in at least four ways. It is:

- **More diverse,** involving a wider variety of institutions, instruments, and sources of support.

- *More entrepreneurial,* moving beyond "grant-making," the giving of resources, to capture the possibilities for greater leverage that comes from adopting an investment orientation, focusing more heavily on measurable results, and generating a blend of economic, as well as social, returns.

- *More global,* engaging problems on an international scale and applying models developed in cross-national settings.

- *More collaborative,* interacting explicitly not only with the broader civil society sector, but also with new social ventures serving the "bottom of the pyramid," as well as with a broad array of private financial institutions and government agencies.

A new paradigm is emerging on the frontiers of philanthropy and social investment.

The result, as outlined in Table 1.1, is a new paradigm emerging on the frontiers of philanthropy and social investing. Where traditional philanthropy relied chiefly on individuals, foundations, and corporate philanthropy programs, the new frontiers of philanthropy engage a broad assortment of private financial institutions, including banks, pension funds, insurance companies, investment advisors, specialized investment funds, and foundations that function as philanthropic banks. Whereas traditional philanthropy concentrated mostly on operating revenue, the new frontiers concentrate far more heavily on investment capital, which funds long-term development. Whereas traditional philanthropy channels its assistance almost exclusively to nonprofit organizations, the new frontiers support as well a wide assortment of social enterprises, cooperatives, and other hybrid organizations. Whereas traditional philanthropy brings a charity perspective to its work, focusing exclusively, or at least chiefly, on social return, actors on the new frontiers of philanthropy

Table 1.1
The *New Frontiers of Philanthropy* paradigm

Philanthropy = "The provision of private resources for social or environmental purposes."

TRADITIONAL PHILANTHROPY	NEW FRONTIERS OF PHILANTHROPY
Foundations, individuals	**Individual and institutional investors**
Operating income	**Investment capital**
Grants	**Diverse financial instruments / capital tranches**
Nonprofits	**Nonprofits + Social ventures**
Social return	**Social + financial return**
Limited leverage	**Expanded leverage**
Output focus	**Outcome focus / metrics**

bring an investment orientation, focusing on social *and* financial return and seeking to build self-sustaining systems that bring permanent solutions. Whereas traditional philanthropy mobilizes a relatively small share of its own resources, the new frontiers of philanthropy leverage the deeper reservoirs of resources resident in the private capital markets. And whereas traditional philanthropy has historically tended to be satisfied with *output* measures, the new frontiers put greater emphasis on reliable *outcome* metrics.

To be sure, these differences are hardly universal. What is more, the changes are far from fully developed. But neither are they trivial. Indeed, as reflected in Figure 1.2, a complex social-purpose finance ecosystem is emerging to channel funds from banks, pension funds, insurance companies, foundations, high net worth individuals, and others through a variety of social-impact investment organizations, support institutions, and new types of grantmakers, to an increasingly diverse set of nonprofits, social ventures, social cooperatives, and related organizations to achieve poverty alleviation, environmental improvement, improved health and environment, strengthened civil society organizations, and improved life chances.

Microfinance, perhaps the earliest manifestation of this phenomenon of mobilizing private investment capital for social purposes, is now a mature $65 billion industry with its

Figure 1.2
The *New Frontiers of Philanthropy* Ecosystem

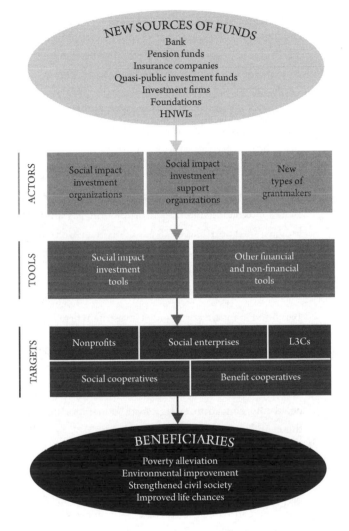

own trade association, research arm, network of "retail" outlets, secondary markets, and access to global capital markets through rated bond issues. And it is just getting started: recent estimates place its *potential* market north of $250 billion.[6]

But microfinance is just one component of the burgeoning financial ecosystem emerging on the new frontiers of philanthropy, broadly conceived. Hundreds of investment funds like the one featured in the African Agricultural Capital Fund vignette outlined above have surfaced around the world and found investors willing to take a chance on them.

- Aavishkaar International, for example, incorporated in Singapore but operating in India, raised an initial $18 million for an Indian microfinance investment fund in 2008. It then proceeded to assemble an additional $14 million more by January 2009 to support promising Indian micro, small, or medium-sized companies operating in the agriculture, dairy, healthcare, education, and renewable energy fields in rural or semiurban areas of the country.[7]

- The Grassroots Business Fund, an offshoot of the World Bank's International Finance Corporation, has similarly built a robust portfolio of $8.5 million in investments and technical assistance engagements supporting small and medium-sized businesses serving low-income populations in India, Africa, and Latin America.[8]

- Bamboo Finance, a commercial investment firm based in Switzerland, manages another US$250 (unless otherwise noted, dollar amounts reported are in US dollars) million of investments in a range of small companies providing access to affordable housing, healthcare, education, energy, livelihood opportunities, water, and sanitation on three continents.[9]

- The Small Business Investment Funds, initially an affiliate of CARE, the international development agency, has invested $378 million in 338 small and midsized companies across 22 emerging markets.[10] Indeed, according to author Lisa Richter in Chapter 2 of the companion volume, such social and environmental oriented investment funds may already number 3,000 around the world and may already have US$300 billion in assets under management.

A commercial revolution appears to be underway around the world at…the "bottom of the pyramid."

For these investment funds to do their work, of course, they must find not only invest*ors*, but also invest*ees*—promising enterprises, whether for-profit or nonprofit, serving social and environmental purposes in a way that yields revenue as well as social good. And finding them they are. Indeed, a commercial revolution appears to be underway around the world at what University of Michigan professor C. K. Prahalad brilliantly termed the "bottom of the pyramid," the base of the world's income scale where the vast majority of the world's population lives.[11] Inventive entrepreneurs are finding ways to transform this population into avid consumers of solar panels, cell phones, eyeglasses, reusable sanitary napkins, and dozens of other basic commodities while also creating opportunities for them to become proprietors and wage earners in artisan shops, small-scale agricultural businesses, and marketing ventures of various sorts. The result is evident in the appearance of firms such as Peru's Agrícola Viñasol (AVSA), an agricultural company created in 2001 as the commercial arm of a Peruvian NGO to help small farmers improve and market their fruit and vegetable products; or Jaipur Rugs, which works with 10,000 low-income weavers and spinners in India to upgrade their production methods, secure healthcare, and market their products; or Zara Solar, which has enabled thousands of low-income Tanzanian families to switch from polluting kerosene stoves to cheaper and cleaner solar-powered ones.[12] (For an illustration of the range of fields in which such social entrepreneurs have surfaced see Table 1.2.)

It is now necessary for these concepts to make the jump to broader strata of participants and observers.

While the changes under way are inspiring and by no means trivial, however, they remain scattered and largely uncharted in any systematic fashion. Individual practitioners typically have a handle on one or another of the relevant innovations, but the full scope of the changes has yet to be visualized, let alone pulled together and examined in a systematic way. Even the terminology used to depict these developments is in flux. Established terms such as "program-related investments"

Table 1.2
Acumen Fund investments, by portfolio type

Agriculture	(Health Con't)
BASIX Krishi Samruddhi Limited (India)	Drishtee (India)
GADCO Coöperatief (Ghana)	First Micro Insurance Agency Pakistan
Global Easy Water Products (India)	Insta Products (Kenya)
Gulu Agricultural Development Company (Uganda)	LifeSpring (India)
Jassar Farms (Pakistan)	Pagatech (Nigeria)
Juhudi Kilimo (Kenya)	PVRI (India)
Micro Drip (Pakistan)	Sproxil (Nigeria)
National Rural Support Program (Pakistan)	UHEAL (Kenya)
Microfinance Bank (Pakistan)	VisionSpring (India)
Virtual City (Kenya)	Voxiva (India)
Western Seed (Kenya)	Ziqitza Health Care Limited (India)
Education	**Housing**
Edubridge (India)	Kashf Foundation (Pakistan)
Hippocampus Learning Centres (India)	Jamii Bora (Kenya)
Energy	Kashf Foundation (Pakistan)
d.light design (India)	Kashf Holdings Private Limited (Pakistan)
Husk Power Systems (India)	Medeem (Ghana)
Orb Energy (India)	Saiban (Pakistan)
Health [a]	**Water**
A to Z Textile Mills (Tanzania)	Ecotact (Kenya)
Botanical Extracts EPZ Limited (Kenya)	GUARDIAN (India)
Books of Hope (Kenya)	Pharmagen Healthcare Ltd (Pakistan)
BroadReach (Kenya)	Spring Health (India)
Circ MedTech (Rwanda)	WaterHealth International (India)
DART (Kenya)	

[a] See Carmody et al. 2011, 66, for descriptions of these businesses.
Source: Acumen Fund homepage, accessed August 18, 2012, http://acumenfund.org.

(PRIs), "mission investing," "market-rate investments," all of which tended to apply narrowly to foundations, have recently been superseded by the term "impact investing," which itself covers only a portion of the emerging field and involves its own significant ambiguities.[13]

What is more, much of the extant literature on these developments takes the form of quasi "gray material," available only in limited editions to a restricted audience. Largely lacking have been materials that can take the changes underway out to a broader audience and that can penetrate the sizable academic universe training nonprofit managers, social entrepreneurs, business leaders, bankers, investment managers, corporate social responsibility officers, and public policy experts. For the new approaches to philanthropy and social investing to achieve the impact of which they are capable, it will be necessary for these concepts to make the jump to broader strata of participants and observers. Even early innovators have come to recognize this point, arguing, as two of them recently put it, that the "challenge now is to bring this [impact investment] perspective from the fringe to the mainstream," which will require "a new generation of…communicators" who can "absorb the lessons from visionary practice and communicate them effectively to much wider audiences."[14]

The Objective and Game Plan of this Volume

The purpose of this monograph, and of the companion volume for which it serves as the introduction, is to address this challenge, to provide a clear and accessible road map to the full range of important new developments taking place on the frontiers of philanthropy and social investment, and thereby broaden awareness of them, increase their credence and traction, and make it possible to maximize the benefits they can generate while acknowledging the limitations and challenges they also face.

The result, in this volume, is the first comprehensive overview of the new actors and tools transforming philanthropy and social investment, the factors giving rise to them, and the steps needed to promote their further development. Readers who find this overview of interest can then turn to the companion volume, entitled *New Frontiers of Philanthropy*, to dig more deeply into the functions of the new actors and the operational dynamics of the various new tools.[15]

It must be emphasized, however, that in exploring the "new frontiers" of philanthropy we are not in any way minimizing the critical role that traditional philanthropy continues to play, or the enormous contributions that existing philanthropic institutions continue to make. Indeed, as will become clear, the creation of the new frontiers has itself not only resulted in important part from groundwork laid by traditional philanthropic actors, but also opened an important new role for these traditional institutions to perform, a role that a number of them have come to recognize and seize.

Three analytical distinctions … shape the structure of this book.

To make sense of these developments, we have made three analytical distinctions that shape the structure of this book and of the companion volume it introduces. First, the book draws a basic distinction between the *actors* that are surfacing in what I am calling the new frontiers of philanthropy, and the *tools* that these actors are utilizing. This distinction is dictated by the extraordinary explosion of activity in this new "philanthropic space" and the confusion that has consequently resulted in sorting out who is doing what. Since any particular actor can utilize a variety of tools, this distinction is crucial to clarifying what is going on.

Second, within each of these groupings I have attempted to differentiate a manageable set of distinctive categories into which to sort the enormous variety of both actors and tools that has surfaced, drawing, where possible, on existing capital-market typologies. Generally speaking, the actors are differentiated according to the functions they are performing. Thus, some are assembling or aggregating capital for deployment into social-purpose activities, others are providing secondary markets or exchanges to allow investors to enter or exit the space, and still others are prospecting for promising ventures or offering specialized technical assistance to such entities. To be sure, because this field is still in its infancy, the degree of specialization that has been attained remains limited, which means that a single actor may be performing a

---

Box 1.1

Calvert Foundation: A Multi-tasking Social-Impact Investment Firm

The Calvert Foundation, launched in 1995, performs a variety of functions in the social impact investing arena. In particular, it

- Manages close to $200 million in social-impact investments;
- Markets a Community Investment Note product to social investors:
- Operates a registered investment advisory service; and
- Created its own donor advised fund, since spun off as a separate entity.

Source: Personal interview, Shari Berenbach, April 29, 2013.

---

variety of roles or utilizing a multitude of tools (see Box 1.1). Even so, it is impossible to make sense of this field without drawing some meaningful distinctions among the basic functions being performed (the actors) and the types of instruments being used (the tools).

A description of these new actors and tools would be incomplete without addressing [the] important cross-cutting issues [they face]...or without acknowledging the critical role that traditional philanthropy continues to play.

Finally, the emergence of these new actors and tools has encountered a number of obstacles and raised a number of cross-cutting issues that also need to be addressed. A description of these new actors and tools would be incomplete without addressing these important obstacles and issues and the dilemmas they pose for the field.

More specifically, this volume pursues four principal tasks:

- First, *descriptive*—to introduce readers to the major types of actors and tools that have taken shape on the

new frontiers of philanthropy and identify some of
their distinctive and novel features. As will become
clear, I identify 11 more or less distinct types of such
actors and eight major types of "new" tools, though
I recognize that others may sort the chaos differently
and the dynamism at work will likely yield additional
types of both actors and tools as the frontiers
expand.

- Second, *analytical*—to explain why this extraordinary
  proliferation of actors and tools is surfacing at this
  point in time and hence what the prospects are for its
  continued development.

- Third, *normative*—to acknowledge some of the
  challenges and risks that these developments also
  bring with them and the steps that have so far been
  taken to address them.

- Fourth, *prescriptive*—to identify the steps that are
  still needed to capture the substantial benefits these
  developments promise while avoiding the risks that
  they also pose.

[This] volume pursues four principal tasks: descriptive, analytical, normative, and prescriptive.

To accomplish these tasks, the discussion here falls naturally
into five chapters in addition to this introduction. Chapter 2
examines the extraordinary array of new *actors* that have
come to populate "philanthropic space" broadly conceived.
Included here are capital aggregators, secondary markets,
social stock exchanges, foundations as philanthropic banks,
enterprise brokers, and several more. Chapter 3 then examines the various *tools* being deployed by these actors. Many of
these are tools that have functioned in the worlds of business
and government for decades but are just gaining acceptance
in the worlds of philanthropy and social investment—tools
like loans, loan guarantees, other credit enhancements, equity
investments, bonds, responsible investing and purchasing,

and securitization. Others are truly novelties, such as "social-impact bonds," prizes, and crowd sourcing.

In Chapter 4 attention turns to the question of why these new frontiers of philanthropy are emerging, and emerging now. To do so, the chapter identifies a set of both "demand factors" and "supply factors" that seem to be propelling these developments. Chapter 5 then zeroes in on a number of obstacles and challenges that confront this field. Included here are limitations in the availability of investment-ready deals, challenges in making good on the field's commitment to measuring social and environmental impact, and concerns over the potential normative and distributional consequences of the shift of control over support for social and environmental purposes from governments and charitable institutions to private investment sources. Finally, Chapter 6 takes up the question of steps that are still needed to advance this field, and address the various risks it faces. Taken together, the result is the first comprehensive account of the new actors and tools operating on the frontiers of philanthropy—deepening the knowledge base from which to inform, educate, train, and responsibly promote this new mode of social-purpose activity.

A Word about Terminology

Before turning to the first of these tasks, however, it is necessary to say a word about terminology. As already noted, the field of action covered by this volume is already a terminological wasteland, strewn with a substantial number of defeated or discarded terms. As one early adventurer on this frontier put it recently, "[When] I started working in this space in 2002 I was a PRI maker; then I became a social investor; mission investor was in there; and now I'm an impact investor; but [my work] has pretty much stayed the same."[16] Under the circumstances it is incumbent on us to be clear about how we are using certain crucial terms and why.

New Frontiers of Philanthropy

We begin, naturally enough, with the headline term we have used for the title of this book: "new frontiers of philanthropy." No doubt this term will encounter its own pushback from some quarters, and on two different grounds. In the first place, there are those who draw a sharp distinction between "philanthropy" and social-purpose "investing," viewing philanthropy as an old-fashioned term conjuring up Lady Bountiful images of paternalistic charity dispensed to homeless orphans—not quite the image sought by the new breed of investment-oriented, metrics-driven "philanthro-capitalists" and "impact investors."[17] What is more, there will be those who question whether the "new frontiers" are all that new. After all, as we note in Chapter 2's discussion of the foundations now functioning as "philanthropic banks," the use of nongrant forms of assistance to promote social purposes—the key feature of this type of actor—was pioneered more than 200 years ago by Benjamin Franklin, who established a charity that provided loans to indigent artisans.

We use the term "philanthropy" in its most basic...meaning: that is, as *the provision of private resources for social or environmental purposes*.

Nevertheless, I am convinced that "new frontiers of philanthropy" is an apt description of the topic of this monograph, and of the fuller volume that accompanies it, certainly compared to any of the likely alternatives. For one thing, the phenomena that we include within the ambit of this volume embrace more than the new forms of social investing that have come to be known as "impact investing." Also included are such developments as responsible investing and purchasing, prizes, crowd sourcing, and various types of giving and investing collaboratives. Perhaps more centrally, we use the term "philanthropy" in its most basic and broadest meaning: that is, as fundamentally *the provision of private resources for social or environmental purposes*.[18] The form in which these resources are delivered is thus not as crucial in this definition of philanthropy as the auspices under which they flow (i.e., they are private) and the purposes towards which they are directed (i.e., they are significantly social or environmental). In this sense, the social-purpose finance that is a principal focus of this book fits well within the field of philanthropy so conceived.

At the same time, while many of the phenomena covered here may not be new to the world, most are new to social and environmental purposes or are operating at a scale in this field that has not been seen before. Thus, for example, some forms of insurance, such as burial insurance, have been available to the poor for a long time. What is new is the marketing of microinsurance products by private, for-profit insurance companies to meet the health, crop, or disaster insurance needs of the poor at prices they can afford. Similarly, capacity-building has been available to nonprofit organizations for several decades. But instead of focusing on the traditional topics of board development, fundraising, and accounting systems, the new frontier of social-purpose capacity-building is focusing on scaling up promising ventures, establishing earned-income streams, and tapping into various forms of investment capital. Finally, even donor-advised funds, a relatively new form of charitable instrument, have been around for several decades in the US. What is new is the emergence and rapid expansion of corporate-originated charitable funds offering donors the opportunity to operate their donor-advised funds through offshoots of the for-profit investment firms that manage their core investments.

All of these are developments that have attained meaningful scale in the past two decades, some in the past five years. But all of them involve the mobilization and distribution of private resources for social or environmental purposes, which is the essence of philanthropy.

Using the term "philanthropy"... also has the virtue of reminding us that, though these activities are... expected to generate a [profit], the fundamental objective remains "social" in the full dictionary meaning of that term.

Using the term "philanthropy" to depict these developments is not only technically correct, however. It also has the virtue of reminding us that, though these activities are engaging private businesses and often utilizing forms of assistance that are expected to generate a financial return, the fundamental objective remains "social" in the full dictionary meaning of that term as "of or having to do with human beings living together as a group in a situation in which their dealings with one another affect their common welfare."[19] Only in this way will we avoid the peril that two early champions of these developments had in mind when they warned that the activities on the frontiers of philanthropy could be made "too easy" if the definition of social and environmental impact becomes "so loose and diluted," or, I would add, so muted "as to be virtually meaningless."[20]

Social-Impact Investing

For this reason also, we have chosen to introduce a slight adjustment to the term of art that has been advanced in much of the available literature to depict what in many respects is the central beachhead on the new frontiers of philanthropy—namely, the mobilization of private investment capital for social and environmental purposes. That term is "impact investing." This term grew out of a series of meetings convened by the Rockefeller Foundation in the mid-2000s as part of its effort to rally private investment houses, and the private investment capital they help direct, into support for the burgeoning social enterprises emerging in both developed and developing countries around the world. Existing terms, such as "social investing," or "program-related investing," or "mission-related investing," or "socially responsible investing," were perceived as being too soft, too closely associated with foundations and philanthropy, too broad, or too passive to appeal to the hardheaded managers of private investment capital. What is more, they were perceived to be incapable of passing muster as a distinct "asset class" around which a new line of investment business could be organized.

The [impact investing] term itself provides little clue about what the content of such "positive impact" is supposed to be.

To their credit, the inventors of the "impact investing" terminology came up with a brilliant solution that served this purpose well. The problem is that the solution may have served this purpose too well, opening the door to precisely the danger that the 2009 Monitor Institute Report warned against: that is, leaving the underlying concept "so loose and diluted" as to make it "virtually meaningless." Although advocates of impact investing regularly emphasize that impact investments are "investments intended to create positive impact beyond financial return,"[21] the term itself provides little clue about what the content of such "positive impact" is supposed to be or what the standard for recognizing its presence is. It thus implicitly puts the emphasis on the idea of investment return rather than on the idea of social and environmental benefit.

Nor does a recent book on impact investing by two leaders in the field do much to clarify the matter. There we learn that "all organizations, for-profit and nonprofit alike, create value that consists of economic, social, and environmental components. All investors, whether market rate, charitable, or some mix of the two, generate all three forms of value."[22] Indeed, one recent publication on the topic goes so far as to define the term "impact" in "impact investment" as "a meaningful change in economic, social, cultural, environmental and/or political conditions due to specific actions and behavioral changes by individuals, communities, and/or society as a whole."[23]

But if all organizations and all investors create "positive impact," and if the term "impact" in "impact investment" consists of any "meaningful change," regardless of its direction or content, how are we to differentiate "impact investors" from plain vanilla investors? The answer, it appears, hinges on "intention," particularly the intention of investees, and on the attention that investors pay to "the blended value returns" reflected in serious impact reporting.[24] But "intention" is notoriously difficult to assess and, as the 2009 Monitor report on impact investing acknowledges, there is "reason to be skeptical" about social and environmental impact measurement systems because "the existing financial markets and incentives create major pull toward 'greenwashing' and dilution of standards...as asset managers seek to respond to growing client interest in impact investing without wanting to take on the long and difficult work of ensuring investment impact."[25]

Already the field has developed a set of impact measures that are so numerous that they begin to resemble those prizes in grade-school contests designed to ensure that every child comes home a winner. No wonder some skeptics have begun to worry that the definition of "impact investing" is coming to resemble "a dog's breakfast,"[26] while others have insisted on adding an adjective like "community" in front of the term to clarify the impacts that the investments are expected to make.[27]

To avoid a similar charge of vagueness, our approach in this volume follows this latter course. Taking our cue from the observation of Bugg-Levine and Emerson that "impact investing for blended value unites the power of business with the purpose of philanthropy,"[28] we suggest that the term for depicting this phenomenon should give equal weight to both sides of this equation. Hence we use the term "social and environmental impact investing," or just "social-impact investing" for short, to refer to it in order to place equal emphasis on the financial and the social or environmental effects these investments are supposed to produce.[29]

Whether an investment can be judged to serve a social purpose can be determined by how it affects any of three crucial factors.

Social Purpose

If we propose to attach the term "social" to the term being used more generally to depict a significant component of the activity on the new frontiers of philanthropy, it is obviously necessary to clarify what we have in mind by it. Fundamentally, therefore, this book takes social-impact investments to be investments that significantly seek to generate "social value," that is, to *promote the health, well-being, and quality of life of a population, particularly disadvantaged segments of that population; encourage the free expression of ideas; or foster tolerance.* Even so, opinions can differ about what truly counts as a "social-impact investment." For example, some observers consider an investment to serve a social purpose if it is made in a disadvantaged area, regardless of who the beneficiaries are, whereas others argue that "[t]he fact that an investment is made in a poor country is not sufficient to qualify as an impact investment."[30]

For our purposes here, whether an investment can be judged to serve a social purpose can be determined by how it affects any of three crucial factors: first, the *population assisted* by it, particularly whether it is a disadvantaged population in some significant sense; second, the *production process* it supports, particularly whether it explicitly involves the employment and training of a disadvantaged or excluded population or reduces the environmental impact of the production; and third, the *goods or services* produced, for example, whether they have inherent environmental advantages.

Investment Capital versus Operating Income

One other terminological distinction about which it will be important to be clear is that differentiating *capital* from *operating revenue* in any enterprise, whether for-profit or nonprofit. Much of the discussion of the financing of social-purpose organizations, particularly that centered on nonprofit organizations, has focused on *operating revenue*, which is the income that organizations use to run their ongoing annual operations. This money typically comes in part from individual and foundation gifts, from government grants and contracts, and from fees for service.[31]

Investment capital is in many senses the life-blood of an organization.

The resources flowing to social-purpose organizations from most, though not all, of the actors on the new frontiers of philanthropy, however, are of a different sort. They take the form of *investment capital*, which is revenue that may contribute to operating income in the future, but fundamentally goes to build long-term organizational capacity and capabilities through the purchase of such things as equipment, facilities, skills, and strategic planning that are expected to serve the organization over the longer haul (see Box 1.2).

Investment capital, too, can come from many different sources and take many different forms. Some can even come

```
┌─────────────────────────────────────────────┐
│                                             │
│  Box 1.2                                    │
│  Investment Capital versus Operating        │
│  Revenue                                    │
│                                             │
│  "Operating revenue allows an organisation  │
│  to deliver defined outputs or outcomes. It │
│  covers day-to-day activities, regular      │
│  service provision and ongoing proj-        │
│  ects. It often takes the form of payments  │
│  for contracted services, grants and        │
│  donations."                                │
│     "Investment capital provides finance    │
│  to build an organisation's long-term       │
│  capacity to achieve its social mission."   │
│                                             │
│  Source: Adapted from UK Big Society Capital,│
│  http://www.bigsociety                      │
│  capital.com/what-social-investment.        │
│                                             │
└─────────────────────────────────────────────┘
```

from gifts, as when a wealthy patron gives a work of art to a museum or donates the resources to construct a building at a university. More commonly, however, investment capital comes in one or both of two other forms: (a) *debt*—that is, loans, or the proceeds of a bond sale, which is a type of loan; or (b) *equity*, the purchase of an ownership, or equity, stake in an organization. In both cases, the providers of investment capital typically require something in return for their investment— payment of principal plus interest in the case of debt; and an ownership stake and payment of a share of whatever profits or surplus the investee might earn in the case of equities.

Investment capital is in many senses the lifeblood of an organization because it is what allows the organization to grow. However, investment capital has historically been hard for social-purpose organizations to secure. For one thing, if they are nonprofits, they cannot accept *equity investments*, per-haps the most attractive form of investment capital because it is essentially free. This is so because equity investors do not have to be paid back unless a firm earns a profit and pays dividends or its shares rise in price. But nonprofits are pro-hibited from paying dividends to their investors or owners and cannot sell shares of their ownership to outside investors. This makes them unable to tap equity investments without special arrangements, increasingly known as *quasi-equity*.

Bond revenue is also typically off the table for social-purpose organizations because, as will become clear below, and more fully in the companion volume, *New Frontiers of Philanthropy*, it is hardly economical to issue bonds for denominations much below $50 million, a threshold that leaves all but the largest social-purpose organizations, such as universities and hospitals, waiting at the altar. This leaves *loans*, but due to the perceived riskiness of social-purpose revenue streams, social-purpose organizations often have to pay premium rates for the debt they take on. Reflecting this, a survey of US nonprofit human service, community development, and arts organizations conducted by the Johns Hopkins Nonprofit Listening Post Project found that 80–90 percent of surveyed organizations in these fields reported a need for investment capital to acquire technology, purchase or renovate facilities, or develop new programs, but fewer than 40 percent reported success in securing the needed capital (see Figure 1.3).[32]

When asked what experiences they have recently had securing investment capital from various sources, moreover, over 90 percent of these organizations reported finding it

Figure 1.3
US Nonprofit Capital Needs and Success in Securing Capital, 2006

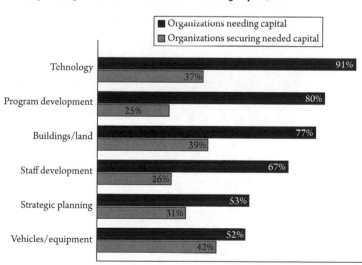

PERCENT OF ORGANIZATIONS

Source: Lester M. Salamon and Stephanie Geller, "Investment Capital: The New Challenge for American Nonprofits," *Communiqué No. 5* (Baltimore: Johns Hopkins Nonprofit Listening Post Project, 2006). http://ccss.jhu.edu. Reprinted with permission.

Figure 1.4
US Nonprofit Difficulty Accessing Investment Capital from Various Sources, 2006

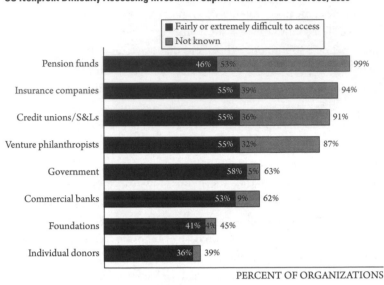

■ Fairly or extremely difficult to access
□ Not known

Pension funds	46% 53%	99%
Insurance companies	55% 39%	94%
Credit unions/S&Ls	55% 36%	91%
Venture philanthropists	55% 32%	87%
Government	58% 5%	63%
Commercial banks	53% 9%	62%
Foundations	41% 4%	45%
Individual donors	36%	39%

PERCENT OF ORGANIZATIONS

Source: Salamon and Geller, "Investment Capital," 2006. Reprinted with permission.

either fairly or extremely difficult to access the major sources of investment capital in the US economy—pension funds, insurance companies, credit unions, and venture capitalists—or they simply had no experience or knowledge of how to approach these sources, leaving them dependent on commercial banks and foundations (see Figure 1.4).[33]

A principal objective of the developments that are the focus of this book and its companion volume is to remedy this dilemma by opening new streams of investment capital for a broad range of social- and environmental-purpose organizations. Against this background, it is therefore possible to turn now to look at what these developments are.

Chapter 2

Scouting Philanthropy's New Frontier I: New Actors

To travel successfully through any new frontier, it is helpful to have at least a basic map of the terrain and some way to identify the types of wildlife that might be encountered along the way. Unfortunately, the new frontier of philanthropy has so far been a largely uncharted territory covered with underbrush and populated by a variety of unfamiliar life-forms. A central objective of this monograph, and of the fuller volume that is a companion to it, is to provide a more coherent guide for those who are contemplating entry into this territory but need a bit more clarity about what they are likely to encounter before venturing forth. Accordingly, as noted previously, and as reflected in Figure 2.1, we have found it helpful to divide the philanthropic frontier into two major regions: the region of the *actors* and the region of the *tools*. The region of the *actors* contains the many new institutions that have come to occupy what we have termed philanthropic space. Although there is enormous diversity among these actors, it is possible to discern some clustering into nearly a dozen more or less identifiable "tribes." Similarly, the region of the *tools* houses the instruments available to these actors to do their work. Eight types of such instruments are identified, ranging from loans and credit enhancements to new types of grants.

Unfortunately, the new frontier of philanthropy has so far been a largely uncharted territory.

The purpose of this chapter and the one that follows is to provide a basic introduction to these various actors and tools. Because most visitors to this new frontier are likely to encounter the new actors in all their variety first, we begin with them. Interestingly, what even the most cursory visit to this frontier makes clear is that while this territory is hardly fully settled, neither is it totally uninhabited.

To the contrary, it is already home to some remarkable life-forms.

The new frontier of philanthropy ... is already home to some remarkable life-forms.

As suggested in Figure 2.1, these life forms can be grouped into three types. The first are essentially new types of financial investment institutions that have emerged to move capital within the newly emerging social-impact investment market. Included here are five types of entities with names quite different from those of traditional philanthropic institutions: they are "capital aggregators," secondary markets, social stock exchanges, quasi-public investment funds, and a special set of foundations functioning as "philanthropic banks." The second group consists of actors that supply various forms of support to these new social-impact financial institutions. Included here are "enterprise brokers," new types of "capacity builders," and a variety of supportive infrastructure

Figure 2.1
Actors and Tools on the New Frontiers of Philanthropy

TYPES OF ACTORS

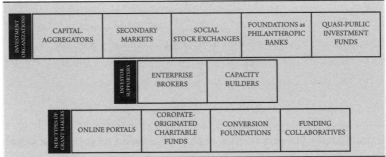

TYPES OF TOOLS

SOCIAL IMPACT INVESTMENT TOOLS	LOANS/CREDIT ENHANCEMENTS	BONDS	SECURITIZATION	EQUITY INVESTMENTS	SOCIAL IMPACT BONDS
OTHER TOOLS		INSURANCE	SOCIAL INVESTING & PURCHASING	PRIZES, CROWD-SOURCING	

organizations. Finally, there are a variety of other actors that remain focused on the more traditional philanthropic tool of grants but are doing so in novel ways. Included here are corporate-originated charitable funds, conversion foundations, online portals and exchanges, and funding collaboratives. Let us examine each of these groupings in more detail.

Social-Impact Investment Institutions

Given the emphasis that the new frontiers of philanthropy are putting on leveraging new sources of investment capital for social and environmental purposes, the natural starting point for a Cook's tour of this frontier region is with the new financial entities that have surfaced to tap and channel these sources. As noted previously, five broad types of new actors in particular deserve attention here.

Easily one of the most crucial of the new actors on the frontiers of philanthropy are ... *capital aggregators*.

Capital Aggregators

Easily one of the most crucial sets of these actors are social-impact *capital aggregators*. These are the organizations that assemble capital for ultimate investment in social-purpose organizations. This function is necessary because only high net worth individuals (HNWIs) are in a position efficiently to invest their resources directly, and even they do not often do so exclusively. Most people with money to invest therefore do so indirectly, through some kind of institution or fund, which aggregates the funds from different investors and finds suitable outlets for them, or provides a market through which capital market actors can conduct trades.

While such institutions are widespread in the standard capital markets in the form of investment firms, mutual funds, and bond and equity funds, they have long been scarce or nonexistent in the social-purpose investment arena, leaving the capital needs of social-purpose organizations to be funded, if at all, by governments, foundations, wealthy individuals, and commercial banks. But this has changed significantly over the past 40 years, and even more dramatically over the past 10 years, much of it with government encouragement.

The US was an early innovator in this arena, beginning with the creation of a network of federally financed community development corporations in the 1960s, a series of state-government-stimulated equity funds to promote job creation in distressed regions beginning in the late 1960s and into the 1970s and 1980s,[1] and a number of supportive federal tax and other policies designed to encourage the flow of private investment capital into low-income housing and community redevelopment.[2] With the invention and spread of microcredit through the work of individuals like Mohammed Yunnus, and the growing recognition, helped along by C. K. Prahalad, of the "profits at the bottom of the pyramid," moreover, the number of capital aggregators focusing on social-purpose investments has accelerated.

As befits their varied origins, social-purpose capital aggregators come in many shapes and sizes and draw on a variety of sources of capital, including high net worth individuals, foundations, and increasingly in recent years, mainline financial institutions such as pension funds, insurance companies, and global financial service firms like J.P. Morgan Chase, Bank of America, Citibank, and UBS, all of which have been attracted by the opportunity to "do good while doing well" and begun to see in so-called impact investing a promising new "asset class."[3]

Not only do the sources of capital aggregated by these entities vary, but so do the forms in which they make it available to investees. Thus, some funds concentrate on loans or other forms of debt, while others specialize in providing equity in various forms to particular classes of ventures at various stages in their development, from early start-up to financing the leap to sustainability.

Most aggregators focus on a particular market niche or region. Thus, for example, ACCION International focuses on microfinance lending institutions in Third World countries. Reflecting the growth of this field, just one of ACCION's affiliates, Banco Compartamos in Mexico, raised $467 million in an initial public offering of stock in 2007, helping to boost the overall global microfinance industry to over $65 billion under management as of 2010.[4]

Then there are the more than 900 Community Development Finance Institutions in the US focusing on distressed urban and rural communities, including more than 600 community development loan funds, 80 venture capital funds, 290 community development credit unions, and 350 community development banks. These institutions had $50 billion under management as of the end of 2013, generated through a wide assortment of investment instruments, including common or preferred stock in the CDFIs themselves, linked deposits, guarantees of CDFI loans to particular classes of borrowers, or subordinated loans to the CDFIs to strengthen the CDFIs' balance sheets and thus permit them to access other resources.[5]

Social-impact capital aggregators function as middlemen in the social capital market.

Whatever their focus or range of investors, however, all social-impact capital aggregators function as middlemen in the social capital market, reaching out to investors willing to invest their capital in social-purpose activities and in turn locating promising social-purpose ventures in which to place it. Given the different risk and return appetites of investors, however, different capital aggregators can operate at different points in the social capital marketplace. Alternatively, they can assemble capital "stacks," or "structured investment products," like the one mentioned in the vignette that led off this volume, with different layers, or "tranches," each with its own risk-return characteristics, and therefore each with its own potential class of investors.

Observers of the field have therefore begun drawing a distinction between "impact-first" investors, who seek to maximize the social or environmental impact of their investments while maintaining a floor for financial return; and "finance-first" investors, who seek to achieve a higher, risk-adjusted market rate of return while still meeting a threshold of social or environmental impact.[6] Where the respective financial and social-impact "floors" lie for these respective investors can therefore differ considerably. Thus, for *impact-first investors*, the impact threshold may be higher and the financial

Figure 2.2
The Relative Domains of Impact-First and Finance-First Social-Impact Investors

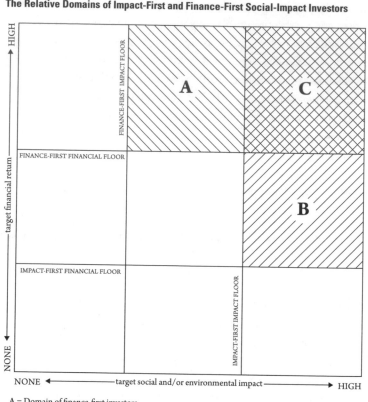

A = Domain of finance-first investors
B = Domain of impact-first investors
C = Domain of both finance-first and impact-first investors

Source: Adapted from Jessica Freireich and Katherine Fulton, *Investing for Social and Environmental Impact*, Monitor Institute, 2009. http://www.monitorinstitute.com/impactinvesting/documents/ InvestingforSocialandEnvImpact_FullReport_004.pdf. Reprinted with permission.

threshold lower than the respective thresholds for financial-first investors, and vice versa. This yields slightly different "sweet spots" for the different investors in the social-impact investment space, as shown in Figure 2.2.[7] Thus, quadrants B and C in Figure 2.2 may work for impact-first investors, while quadrants and A and C are the available locations for finance-first investors.

Not surprisingly, different types of social-impact capital aggregators will operate in these different zones. As a general rule, nonprofit social-impact capital aggregators tend to appeal to investors with an impact-first orientation, frequently individuals or foundations. For their investors, the financial return threshold can be set below where for-profit investors might put it, and they might be willing to accept a higher ratio of risk to return. These investors are therefore highly prized for the kind of structured investment products described above because they will more willingly accept the first-loss grant or guarantee tranches on the bottom of such structured investments, thus absorbing much of the risk and making it possible for profit-oriented private investors to enter deals that would otherwise have little appeal to them.

Typical of this type of nonprofit social-purpose capital aggregator is Acumen Fund, a nonprofit capital aggregator founded in 2001 that has built a robust portfolio of investments supporting "entrepreneurs able to provide critical services [water, health, housing, and energy] at affordable prices to people earning less than four dollars a day" in eight countries of South Asia and East and West Africa—clearly an impact-first objective.[8] The organization goes after "philanthropic capital," which tends to be satisfied with lower return rates or merely return of principal, but still strives to make "disciplined investments intended to yield both financial and social returns" (see Box 2.1).

For-profit capital aggregators are more likely to set the financial return bar higher while still seeking meaningful social returns. Thus, for example, UK-based Bridges Ventures and Dubai-based Willow Impact Investors are both for-profit, social-impact capital aggregators that utilize a private-equity model, attracting funds from investors with more of a risk-adjusted market return expectation.[9]

Whatever their strategy, form, focus, or market niche,

Social-impact capital aggregators have mushroomed in number, size, and diversity over the past decade or more.

however, it seems clear that social-impact capital aggregators have mushroomed in number, size, and diversity over the past decade or more. One indicator of this is the 190 funds already listed on the ImpactBase website created by the Global Impact Investment Network (GIIN),

Box 2.1

Acumen Fund Mission Statement: Changing the Way the World Tackles Poverty

Our mission is to create a world beyond poverty by investing in social enterprises, emerging leaders, and breakthrough ideas.

Our vision is that one day every human being will have access to the critical goods and services they need—including affordable health, water, housing, energy, agricultural inputs and services—so that they can make decisions and choices for themselves and unleash their full human potential. This is where dignity starts—not just for the poor but for everyone on earth.

The Challenge. Tremendous wealth is being created in the world today thanks to globalization and the power of technology and markets. Yet there is a growing gap between rich and poor. Something must be done to extend the benefits of the global economy to the majority of the world's population that lives on less than four dollars a day.

Why Charity Alone isn't the Answer. Poor people seek dignity, not dependence. Traditional charity often meets immediate needs but too often fails to enable people to solve their own problems over the long term. Market-based approaches have the potential to grow when charitable dollars run out, and they must be a part of the solution to the big problem of poverty.

Why the Marketplace Alone isn't the Answer. Very low-income people are too often invisible to businesses and society. Businesses see no significant market opportunity and governments view low-income areas as having insufficient tax revenues to pay for basic services like clean water, healthcare, housing and energy. Building new models that provide these critical services at affordable price—in the face of high costs, poor distribution systems, dispersed customers, limited financing options and, at times, corruption—requires imaginative business solutions and partnerships supported by investors willing to take on a risk/return profile that is unacceptable to traditional financiers.

Changing the Development Paradigm. We believe that pioneering entrepreneurs will ultimately find the solutions to poverty. The entrepreneurs Acumen Fund supports are focused on offering critical services—water, health, housing, and energy—at affordable prices to people earning less than four dollars a day. The key is patient capital. We use philanthropic capital to make disciplined investments—loans or equity, not grants—that yield both financial and social returns. Any financial returns we receive are recycled into new investments. Over time, we have refined the Acumen Fund investment model, built a world-class global team with offices in four countries, and learned what does and does not work in growing businesses that serve low-income people.

Source: Acumen Fund, "About Us," accessed August 12, 2012, http://www.acumenfund.org.

a network of social-impact investors organized by the Rockefeller Foundation and several partners. In addition to the 190 funds listed, this site has attracted 730 accredited investor-subscribers.[10]

More generally, as already noted, Lisa Richter estimates in Chapter 2 of the companion volume to this monograph that the number of capital aggregators may have reached 3,000 internationally, with $300 billion under management.[11] Growth rates of funds under management have been dramatic, moreover. Global investments in clean energy thus grew from US$36 billion in 2004 to $155 billion in 2008 and, despite the financial crisis, still stood at $145 billion at the end of 2009.[12] Between 2004 and 2008, according to Richter, US CDFI investments grew at an annual compound rate of 10 percent a year, global microfinance investments by 20 percent a year, and global clean technology investments by 30 to 40 percent a year.

Nor does it appear that this trend is weakening. One influential report prepared in 2009 by J.P. Morgan Social Finance estimated a global demand for social-impact investments over the ensuing decade ranging from $400.6 billion to nearly $1 trillion in just five fields (housing, rural water supply, maternal health, primary education, and financial services).[13]

What performance data are available on existing

Capital aggregators are both expecting, and so far achieving, return rates on their social-impact investments ... in line with high-performing benchmark equity and debt indexes.

---

social-impact investments suggest, moreover, that investors may have incentives to meet this demand. Thus, for example, drawing on data generated by the CDFI Data Project and the Microfinance Information Exchange, Richter reports that net loss rates were under 1 percent for US CDFIs for the period 2000–2008, that they rose temporarily to 1.78 percent by the end of 2009, but even then remained below the 2.49 percent mortgage "charge-off" rate at regular, non-CDFI, federally insured US banks. Microfinance institutions similarly experience net loan loss rates under 1 percent. More generally, available evidence suggests that capital aggregators are both expecting, and so far achieving, return rates on their social-impact investments, both debt and equity, in line with high-performing benchmark equity and debt indexes, such as the S&P 500, Russell 2000 Growth, PIMCO Total Return, and J.P. Morgan Emerging Markets Bond.[14]

Secondary market operators have also sprung up in the social-purpose arena.

Secondary Markets

While capital aggregators are one important set of financial actors that have surfaced on the new frontiers of philanthropy, they are by no means the only one. A second set consists of social-impact *secondary markets*. These are institutions that purchase the loans originated by capital aggregators, refreshing the capital available to the capital aggregators so they can make additional loans. To do so, the secondary market institutions use a process called "securitization" to bundle the loans into packages and use them as collateral against which to issue bonds on the capital markets.[15]

Secondary markets have long functioned in the regular capital markets, especially in the housing field. Readers familiar with US capital markets will recognize this as the function performed by the Federal National Mortgage Association, lovingly known as "Fannie Mae," originally established as a government corporation to purchase federally guaranteed home mortgages from the originating commercial banks and savings and loans.

This function did not develop in the social-impact investment arena until the late 1980s, however, with the establishment of the US-based Community Reinvestment Fund (CRF), created to support the growing low-income housing and community development market. As detailed by

David Erickson in Chapter 3 of the companion volume to this monograph, CRF initially had to raise its capital through private placements of community development bonds.[16] In 2004, however, it was finally able to issue a bond "rated" by one of the quasi-official rating agencies, Standard and Poor's, which allowed it to attract eight new institutional investors that had previously been unable to invest in CRF bonds because of investment guidelines that prevented them from investing in unrated securities. To date, CRF has purchased over $1.4 billion in community development loans from more than 150 lending organizations located in 46 of the country's 50 states.[17]

By demonstrating the power of securitization and secondary market purchases to inject fresh capital into social-impact investment markets, CRF has stimulated the emergence of additional secondary market institutions in different social-impact fields. For some of these, like CRF, secondary market transactions are their exclusive function, while for others the secondary market activity is an offshoot of a robust loan origination activity. This is the case, for example, with Habitat for Humanity International (HFHI), the well-known international nonprofit that mobilizes volunteers to help low-income families construct homes for themselves. To cover the costs of building supplies and equipment for the houses they help build, HFHI affiliates have approximately $1.4 billion in mortgages outstanding to new homeowners. To allow the affiliates to continue their construction activities, HFHI has developed a secondary market operation called the Flex-Cap Program under which it purchases a portion of these loans from the affiliates using capital it generates from selling investors seven- or ten-year notes backed by the pledged mortgages. Habitat then pays off these notes from the principal and interest payments made by the homeowners. The program has a 100 percent repayment rate and has allowed HFHI to raise $107 million.[18]

Nor are these isolated examples. Partners for the Common Good (PCG), a CDFI founded in 1989 to serve Catholic institutions, recently raised $25.3 million to purchase home mortgages from its affiliates; Blue Orchard, a Swiss microfinance investment fund, raised nearly $200 million to purchase microfinance loans from 21 microfinance investment organizations around the world; and BRAC, the huge Bangladeshi nonprofit development organization, similarly recently raised $180 million in capital to purchase microfinance loans made by its affiliates.[19]

Social stock exchanges are a third class of organizations taking shape on the frontiers of philanthropy.

Social Stock Exchanges

A third class of organizations taking shape on the frontiers of philanthropy brings the concept of a stock exchange to the social and environmental impact investment arena. Social stock exchanges provide a more efficient way for social-impact investors to connect with social ventures seeking capital. Unlike social-impact capital aggregators and secondary-market operators, who must go through the trouble of searching out investors who share their social-impact/risk-return appetites and then market their investment products to them, social stock exchanges simply provide platforms through which dispersed investors can locate social investments in which they are interested. What is more, exchanges provide automatic assurance to such investors that they can exit the investments whenever this becomes necessary or desirable. Of course, for this to be possible, as Shahnaz, Kraybill, and Salamon note in Chapter 4 of the companion volume to this monograph, the exchanges must develop listing rules, standard disclosure requirements for the listed entities, and trading mechanisms that are efficient, accurate, and fraud-proof.[20]

One of the earliest uses of this mechanism in the social-impact arena was in the environmental area. The Chicago Climate Exchange, created in 2003 in anticipation of the hoped-for passage of a "cap and trade" permit system for "carbon emission credits," allowed companies able to achieve emission reductions cheaply to secure tradable credits that they could sell through the exchange to companies for which emission reductions would be far more costly.

Although the 2010 failure of cap-and-trade legislation in the US Congress caused a pullback for the Chicago Climate Exchange, the Kyoto Protocol, which came into effect in 2005, has allowed other emission trading exchanges outside of the US (which did not sign this protocol) to expand well beyond what the Chicago exchange was handling. Thus, the European Climate Exchange, the world's largest, saw its volume expand from 94 million equivalent tons of carbon dioxide in 2005 to 5.3 billion equivalent tons in 2010, and it is only one of 10 such exchanges operating globally. According to the World Bank, overall carbon trading stood at US$142 billion as of 2010, though the global economic slowdown coupled with an overly generous supply of free credits in Europe has caused at least a temporary pullback in trading.[21]

The first social investment "exchange" outside of the climate arena emerged in 2003 in Brazil with the launch of the Bolsa de Valorous Socioambientais (BVSA), or social and environmental investment exchange, though this entity functions more like an online contribution platform than an actual investment vehicle. BVSA screens projects to determine their alignment with the UN Millennium Development Goals, but donors who "invest" in these projects are entitled only to social, but no financial, return.[22]

More ambitious, formalized private placement markets have now surfaced as well. These include Mission Markets in the US, Impact Partners in Singapore, and Artha in India. More ambitious yet are several full-fledged social stock exchanges that are now nearing operational status in a number of locations around the world. These include Social Stock Exchange Ltd (SSE) in the UK, Impact Exchange (iX) in Mauritius, and the Impact Investment Exchange (IIX) in Singapore. The most fully developed at this point appears to be the Mauritius iX entity, which has received formal regulatory approval from the Stock Exchange of Mauritius (SEM) of rules for listing and

trading qualified social- and environmental-purpose enterprises and social-impact investment funds within the SEM
structure but under a separate SEM board. Further, iX
Mauritius has now teamed up with the Singapore Impact
Investment Exchange to work with the SEM to bring iX to
a successful launch by the end of 2013.

**Public-sector organizations have also joined the march toward creating specialized
social-impact investment programs.**

Quasi-public Investment Funds

Public-sector organizations have also joined the march
toward creating specialized social-impact capital investment
programs and facilities. Prominent among these have been
the entries by several of the multinational development banks
such as the World Bank and the Inter-American Development
Bank. Unlike the capital aggregators described earlier,
these institutions essentially pool *public sector* resources for
social-impact purposes.

Thus, for example, the International Finance Corporation
(IFC), an affiliate of the World Bank created to stimulate private business in developing countries, has recently
added a social-impact investment initiative to its portfolio. As just one example, the IFC has funneled $481 mil-
lion to 63 private school projects in developing countries
aimed at supplementing grossly inadequate public school
systems with low-cost private education options. In Kenya,
for example, 23 private schools have received an average of
$300,000 in loans each and 113 others have received advi-
sory support.[23]

The Inter-American Development Bank has similarly
established a Multilateral Investment Fund (MIF) through
which it has also actively entered the social-impact investment field. One recent investment, for example, involved a
$25 million loan and $5 million in equity finance in Mexico's
IGNIA Fund, which helped leverage a total of $102 million
for investments in small and medium-sized enterprises serving those at the base of the pyramid.[24]

Nor are multinational development banks the only public-sector entities developing social-impact investment entities. The UK government has been especially active, and especially inventive, in channeling public, or quasi-public, resources into social-impact investment activity. This has included dedicating proceeds from the UK lottery to the creation of a "foundation of social innovation" called NESTA, and tapping the proceeds of long-dormant and unclaimed bank accounts to seed a sizable, quasi-public, social-impact investment fund called Big Society Capital that is expected to end up with assets approaching £400 million/US$600 million.[25]

A number of charitable foundations have begun functioning as virtual "*philanthropic banks*," ... tapping their core investment assets and going well beyond their traditional reliance on the tool of grants.

Foundations as "Philanthropic Banks"

Finally, a number of charitable foundations have begun moving well beyond the traditional foundation reliance on grants as the chief, or only, form of financial assistance and begun functioning as virtual "philanthropic banks" or social investment funds. Some of these institutions are simply applying social, environmental, and corporate governance (ESG) screens to increased shares of their normal investment decision-making. But a number of others are combining this type of investment screening with more active engagement in the social-impact investment market.[26] This has involved going well beyond the traditional foundation reliance on the tool of grants and utilizing a much wider array of financial instruments—for example, loans, loan guarantees, equity investments, bonds, and bond guarantees. And it has also involved tapping not only their grant budgets but their core investment assets as well, thus challenging the long-standing foundation tradition of keeping separate their two major lines of "business": their "investment business," which has historically been expected to focus single-mindedly on responsibly maximizing investment income in order to support the foundation's charitable activities; and their "grant business," which has historically been expected to focus narrowly on dispensing some share of the resulting proceeds in the form of charitable grants.[27]

A broad array of foundations has begun moving in this direction, ranging from midsized institutions such as the KL Felicitas Foundation, the Babcock Foundation, the Wallace Global Fund, and the Educational Foundation of America to some of the nation's largest foundations, such as the Annie E. Casey Foundation, the Kellogg Foundation, the Kresge Foundation, and the Robert Wood Johnson Foundation, among others. Thus, as detailed by Salamon and Burckart in chapter 5 of the companion to this volume, the KL Felicitas Foundation, created by dot-com entrepreneur Charly Kleissner and his wife, Lisa, has 78 percent of its core assets committed to social-impact investments.[28] The H.B. Heron Foundation in New York, a pioneer in this arena, has 42 percent so invested. Nor is this an exclusively US phenomenon. The Esmee Fairbarn Foundation in the UK and the Fondazione CRT in Italy have joined this parade as well, the latter creating a separate subsidiary, the Fondazione Sviluppo e Crescita (the Development and Growth Foundation) to get around Italian laws limiting the ability of foundations to use their assets in such leveraged ways to support for-profit enterprises.[29]

This expanded foundation experimentation with novel forms of financing is not entirely new, of course. The 1969 US tax law that established the foundation "payout" requirement also opened the door for foundation use of an expanded array of financial instruments through what were called "program-related investments" (PRIs). However, PRIs were conceived as a form of grant funded out of a foundation's 5 percent grant budget. What is more, due to the administrative constraints placed on this vehicle and the general conservatism of foundation financial management, the number of PRI makers out of the more than 75,000 US foundations peaked at 133 in 2004 and dropped back to 120 as of 2007, the year before the US financial meltdown. While these tended to be fairly large institutions, moreover, the overall share of foundation assets devoted to such PRIs has never exceeded 1 percent.[30]

What the new breed of "foundations as philanthropic banks" is doing is reimagining the field by taking the PRI concept to a new level—breeching "the Chinese wall" between the program and investment sides of the foundation house, utilizing a much broader array of financial instruments, and consciously seeking greater leverage from their investments by using their funds to catalyze the flow of private investment capital into social-purpose activities.

A variety of types of service providers has also recently surfaced to assist the capital aggregators.

Social-Impact Investment Support Institutions

To assist the capital aggregators, secondary markets, foundations as philanthropic banks, and quasi-public investment funds that have surfaced in this new social-impact capital market, a variety of types of service providers has also recently surfaced. Three of these in particular deserve special attention here: enterprise brokers, sustainability capacity builders, and new infrastructure organizations.

Enterprise Brokers

One of the most significant of these support entities for the social-impact financial institutions are what might be called "enterprise brokers." Enterprise brokers are individuals or institutions that perform the crucial middleman function of helping capital aggregators identify promising ventures capable of delivering the desired combination of financial and social returns, and helping such ventures find their way to investors with the substantive and financial interests aligned with the ventures' activities and needs.

As described by Hagerman and Wood in Chapter 6 of the companion to this volume, the need for this function arises from the significant transaction costs that exist on both sides of the social-impact investment market as investors and social entrepreneurs search out partnerships that align their respective fields of activity, desired forms of investment, and risk and return profiles across a highly fragmented social-impact investment space.[31] Also at work are the special difficulties of assessing risk in the social-impact arena given the uncertainties of new products being marketed by relatively untested social entrepreneurs to bottom-of-the-pyramid consumers whose market behavior has yet to be fully analyzed.

New *capacity builders* have surfaced focusing on sustainability and scaling.

Capacity Builders

Another function that has expanded and assumed new forms with the growth of social ventures and social-impact investment is that of social venture capacity builders. As noted earlier, capacity builders and technical assistance providers have operated in the nonprofit or social-purpose organization arena for decades. Indeed, nonprofit capacity builders in the US have their own infrastructure organization called the Alliance for Nonprofit Management, a specialized organization called BoardSource to provide advice on the management of boards of directors, and a robust affinity group of foundation supporters known as Grantmakers for Effective Organizations (GEO).

For the most part, however, these existing organizations and consultants have focused on standard organizational management topics such as fundraising, special events, board development, accounting systems, and human resource policies. What characterizes the "new capacity builders" is a considerably different focus. Their objective is organizational *sustainability* and *scaling*. They assist organizations to develop *earned-income strategies*, access the new, nongrant forms of capital now available, and measure social outcomes.[32]

These new capacity builders fall into two broad groups, though there is extensive interaction between the two. One group takes its inspiration from a celebrated 1997 *Harvard Business Review* article that challenged foundations to act more like venture capitalists by taking a more active role in improving the management and operations of the organizations they support.[33] This has given rise to the field of "venture philanthropy" populated by organizations that provide a combination of funding and intensive, "high engagement" technical assistance and organizational development that they either provide themselves or hire outside consultancies to deliver for them. Some of these organizations are traditional foundations like the Edna McConnell Clark Foundation, which has decided to pursue its mission of helping young people from low-income backgrounds become independent through a strategy of making very large grants to a limited number of promising organizations and pouring substantial capacity building assistance into the grantee organizations to ensure their long-term sustainability (see Box 2.2).[34]

Others are regular public charities that have raised funds through other means and similarly use them to provide a combination of capacity-building assistance and funding to targeted ventures. Included here are organizations such

Box 2.2
Edna McConnell Clark Foundation: How We Work

We believe that an effective and efficient way to meet the urgent needs of youth is to make large, long-term investments in nonprofit organizations whose programs have been proven to produce positive outcomes and that have the potential for growth. Our funding consists largely of support for business planning, capacity building and program evaluation, so that grantees can expand while maintaining the quality of their programs, make an impact on the life trajectories of more young people, and eventually become organizationally, programmatically and financially sustainable. Our goal is to help develop a growing pool of organizations that serve thousands more youth each year with proven programs.

Source: "How We Work," Edna McConnell Clark Foundation, accessed May 11, 2013, http://www.emcf.org/how-we-work/.

as New Profit, the Roberts Enterprise Development Fund (REDF), Social Venture Partners (SVP), and Venture Philanthropy Partners (VPP). New Profit, for example, is a 47-person firm founded in 1998 that has raised money from nearly 50 individual and family philanthropists to provide in-depth technical and financial help to 27 promising social ventures that have in turn served over 1.4 million people across the US.[35]

A second group of sustainability capacity builders are classic consultancies that have made a specialty of promoting organizational sustainability but do not themselves provide financial assistance. Some of these are hired by venture philanthropies to deliver the required technical assistance, while others are hired directly by emerging social enterprises or traditional nonprofits wanting to boost their revenues from earned income. Included here are the Bridgespan Group, a dedicated social-purpose consulting firm that grew out of the for-profit Bain Consulting firm; Community Wealth Ventures, a subsidiary of the antihunger organization Share our Strength that focuses on helping organizations develop earned-income strategies; and the Nonprofit Finance Fund, which helps organizations manage their balance sheets.

While venture philanthropy and social venture capacity-builders more generally emerged initially in the US, they have spread far wider. The European Venture Philanthropy Association, for example, has attracted 127 individual and organizational members that share five key features: they have capital to invest; they focus on providing long-term funding to social-purpose organizations, whether nonprofit or for-profit; they are primarily seeking a social, rather than a financial, return; and they take an active role in promoting the "core development" of the organizations they are supporting.[36] (See Box 2.3 for the operating characteristics of "venture philanthropy" as practiced by the members of EVPA.)

Yet another model for capacity-building in the emerging social-venture and social-impact investing space is afforded by The Hub. Launched in London in 2005, The Hub is a

Box 2.3
7 Key Characteristics of European Venture Philanthropy

1. **High engagement**—Hands-on relationships between the social enterprise or nonprofit management and the venture philanthropists.
2. **Organizational capacity-building**—Building the operational capacity of the portfolio organizations, by funding core operating costs rather than individual projects.
3. **Multi-year support**—Supporting a limited number of organizations for 3–5 years, then exiting when organizations supported are financially or operationally sustainable
4. **Non-financial support**—Providing value-added services such as strategic planning to strengthen management.
5. **Involvement of networks**—Providing access to networks enables various and often complementing skill-sets and resources being made available to the investees.
6. **Tailored financing**—Using a range of financing mechanisms tailored to the needs of organizations supported.
7. **Performance measurement**—Placing emphasis on good business planning, measurable outcomes, achievement of milestones and financial accountability and transparency.

Source: European Venture Philanthropy Association. http://www.evpa.eu.com.

network of 4,000 aspiring social entrepreneurs in some 31 chapters around the world, who meet to share experience, contacts, and ideas, and who share workspaces in which to nurture early-stage venture ideas. Separate Hub chapters are free to formulate their own approaches to capacity-building. Thus, for example, Hub Johannesburg runs a Hub Business Clinic that offers twice-monthly skills sessions for social entrepreneurs, while the Hub Bay Area recently launched

Hub Ventures, a structured program that helps a select group of entrepreneurs develop their concepts through mentorship, workshops, and other technical assistance and then awards $75,000 in seed capital for those with the most promising concepts.[37]

A substantial network of social impact *infrastructure organizations* has also emerged.

Infrastructure Organizations

In addition to the entities described above, which all offer essentially "retail" assistance and support to social-impact investors, social entrepreneurs, or mainline nonprofit organizations in new ways, a substantial network of infrastructure organizations has also emerged to support the work of these operating entities at a more macro, or wholesale, level. These entities serve a number of crucial functions for the fields in which they operate: they connect the actors in the field to each other; they popularize and publicize the field and thereby attract newcomers and external support; and they legitimize and strengthen the practice.

The social-impact investing space has provided the most fertile ground for the growth of such infrastructure organizations, with separate entities emerging to service virtually every constituency, and every nook and cranny, of this rapidly developing field. Thus, for example, one of the earliest entrants was the Opportunity Finance Network, created in 1985 to support US community development finance institutions (CDFIs) in their mission of aiding "low-income, low-wealth, and other disadvantaged people and communities join the economic mainstream."[38] Now US CDFIs also have the Community Development Venture Capital Alliance and the National Federation of Community Development Credit Unions. Similarly, "sustainability investors" have the Aspen Network of Development Entrepreneurs (ANDE); socially motivated banks participate in the Global Alliance for Banking Values. Similarly, advocates of "responsible investing" have joined together in the Social Investment Forum (SIF) to promote adherence to the UN Principles for Responsible Investment

(UNPRI), which calls on firms to adhere to responsible environmental, social, and corporate governance (ESG) standards.[39] CGAP, the Consultative Group to Assist the Poor, is a consortium of 33 donors with the common goal to advance access to financial services for the poor.[40] US foundation officials making active use of program-related investments (PRIs) formed the PRI Makers Network to share experiences, develop best practices, and attract other foundations into the fold. As interest grew in other ways to extend the mission-related activities of foundations as well (e.g., through screening endowment investments or strategically voting shares), a new organization emerged called More for Mission, initially headquartered at Boston College. Now these two foundation groupings have come together under the banner of the Mission Investors Exchange.[41] European foundations engaging in social-impact investing and high-engagement grant-making have similarly felt the need for an infrastructure organization, and 130 of them have joined together, as noted earlier, in the European Venture Philanthropy Association. Microfinance investors have also found it useful to build infrastructure organizations to serve their particular needs, giving rise to the Microfinance Investment Exchange and the International Association of Microfinance Investors (IAMFI).

Notwithstanding this profusion of infrastructure organizations, a group of foundations, development agencies, and private financial institutions convened by the Rockefeller Foundation in a series of key gatherings in 2007 and 2008 came to the conclusion that a broader field-building effort was still needed that could bring these various separate initiatives together under a common umbrella and move the field beyond what one pair of authors termed "uncoordinated innovation."[42] The upshot was the launch in 2009 of yet another infrastructure organization called GIIN, the Global Impact Investing Network, but this time with substantial funding from the Rockefeller Foundation, J.P. Morgan, and the United States Agency for International Development. The GIIN was charged with the task of accelerating the development of the social-impact investing industry by creating critical infrastructure, improving practice, establishing a common language, and stimulating field-building research. To do so, it has established an "Investors' Council" made up of leading impact investors from around the world; created so-called Impact Reporting and Investment Standards (IRIS), a broad set of indicators through which social-impact investors can measure the social performance of their investments; established an online database of impact investment funds called "ImpactBase" to facilitate collaboration among funds working in similar fields and geographies; and carried out a variety of outreach efforts to elevate the visibility of the field and encourage its expansion, including research designed to establish social-impact investing as an "asset class" with its own skill requirements, organizational structures, metrics, trade groups, and educational offerings.[43]

New Types of Grant-making Entities

While the previous new actors on the frontiers of philanthropy have all been involved in some aspect of social-impact investing involving nongrant forms of finance, other entities are bringing imaginative new approaches to mobilizing some of the less esoteric forms of charitable activity through such mechanisms as online portals, funding collaboratives, and corporate-originated charitable funds.

Online portals or exchanges make creative use of the new communications technologies to connect donors and investors directly to recipient organizations.

Online Portals and Exchanges

One of the more innovative of these types of entities is a new class of *online portals or exchanges* that are making creative use of the new communications technologies to connect donors and investors directly to recipient organizations and ventures with an immediacy that has not been possible before. These are not just internet service providers that happen to be used to transfer cash, commodities, and volunteering opportunities, however. Rather, they are organizations specifically structured to serve as transfer points between donors and beneficiaries, often with the benefit of elaborate databases and security systems. What is more, they have evolved to handle at least three different types of valued resources: (a) financial resources, including short-term cash and long-term investment capital; (b) commodities, such as computer hardware and software, pharmaceuticals, and food; and (c) services, both paid and volunteer.[44]

As with so much of the activity on the new frontiers of philanthropy, these online portals have mushroomed in number and scale. One recent source identifies over 170 such entities handling charitable giving alone.[45] Just one of these, Network for Good, has generated an estimated half billion dollars of contributions to some 60,000 organizations from its inception in 2001 through early 2011. Kiva, a different type of entity, allows small-scale social entrepreneurs in faraway places to access loans funded through donations from socially oriented investors in the US, western Europe, and elsewhere. From its founding in 2005 through 2012, Kiva has facilitated over $360 million in loans from over 835,000 individuals to nearly 885,000 social entrepreneurs, 82 percent of whom are women, and achieved a repayment rate of nearly 99 percent.[46]

TechSoup Global, another online portal, provides nonprofit organizations access not to cash, but to technology hardware and software contributions for a modest fee. Through late 2010, the organization had distributed $6.6 billion worth of technology products to 133,000 organizations around the world.[47] Volunteer Match performs a similar function for volunteers, operating a huge matchmaking operation to help individuals and businesses with volunteer programs to connect potential volunteers with organizations that need their services. In 2010 alone, VolunteerMatch estimates that its volunteer assignments generated social value worth more than $600 million if organizations had had to pay for the assistance they received from the organization's volunteer placements.[48]

To be sure, these online portals have not yet achieved a scale that rivals mainline contribution mechanisms. What is more, there is valid reason to question whether they are making a net addition to the resources being mobilized for charitable purposes. Nevertheless, as this set of actors has gained traction and visibility they have prompted a wave of innovative newcomers to this field that together are injecting new vibrancy and immediacy into traditional charitable giving and volunteering. Among these relative newcomers are Care2.com, mobilizing social change advocates; Idealist.com, providing job postings in the social-purpose arena; Americares.com, delivering medical supplies; and DonorsChoose, providing assistance to schoolteachers.

Another new set of actors are the huge charitable funds originated by some of the country's largest for-profit investment companies...

Corporate-Originated Charitable Funds

Side by side with the emergence of for-profit social-purpose investment funds has been the appearance of another new set of entities—huge charitable funds originated by some of the country's largest for-profit investment companies, such as Fidelity Investments, Charles Schwab and Sons, and Vanguard. These funds have been set up to manage charitable funds for the investment clients of these firms as well as others. Thirty-two such corporate-originated charitable funds are now in operation in the US alone, with assets of $12 billion, mostly in the form of some 88,000 "donor advised funds." These are pools of charitable resources that are similar to minifoundations, allowing donors to receive charitable tax deductions on the full value of their contributions when they set up the funds, but then permitting them to direct contributions from the funds over their lifetimes.[49]

The first of these funds was founded only in 1991, but in 21 years it has already overtaken the scale of donor-advised funds managed by the country's largest community foundation, which has been in existence for nearly 100 years. By streamlining their back-office and investment functions through service contracts with their originating firms, these entities have posed a significant challenge not only to community foundations but potentially to the continued growth of foundations more generally. Taken together, the 32 corporate-originated funds already manage donor-advised fund assets roughly equivalent to those managed by the country's entire network of over 600 community foundations, which previously held a virtual monopoly on the management of such funds.[50] In the process they have helped to stimulate broader introduction of information-management technology and more sophisticated investment management in the charitable enterprise more generally.[51] While still focused heavily on grant-making, moreover, these entities have begun to experiment with some of the broader financial instruments now penetrating the social investing arena generally.

"Conversion foundations," another type of charitable institution, emerge from the process of privatization of state-owned or -controlled assets.

Conversion Foundations

Yet another type of charitable institution that has made its appearance on the new frontiers of philanthropy is what has come to be called a "conversion foundation." Unlike classical independent foundations, which are normally formed out of the fortunes amassed by individual entrepreneurs, conversion foundations are formed out of the process of privatizing some public or quasi-public asset, a process I have termed "philan-thropication thru. privatization," or "PtP." The asset in question can be a government-owned enterprise, a government-owned building or other property, specialized streams of revenue under government control (e.g., proceeds from state-run lotteries or sales of mineral rights), debt swaps, and conversions of quasi-public organizations such as nonprofits into for-profits.[52]

The emergence of this type of foundation can be traced in important part to the recent neoliberal push to privatize public, or quasi-public, institutions. While the proceeds of such transactions usually find their way into government budgets or, in some celebrated occasions, into the pockets of politicians, it turns out that in a number of cases the proceeds are placed into existing or newly formed foundations and form all or a portion of the assets of such institutions.

One of the earliest examples of this phenomenon was the creation of the Volkswagen Foundation out of the privatization of the Nazi Party–inspired, state-owned Volkswagen Company in the aftermath of the Second World War. The resulting foundation, created in 1960, has become one of the leading foundations in Europe, with assets of $3.5 billion dedicated to the promotion of German science. In the process, the Volkswagen Foundation has served as a role model or template for several other privatization transactions in Germany.[53]

But the Volkswagen case is hardly an isolated example: this alternative use of privatization proceeds has occurred far more frequently than has previously been recognized, yielding significant charitable endowments, some of them quite huge. Indeed, over 500 such "conversion foundations" have been identified around the world, accounting for at least $135 billion in assets, with examples of each of the types of initial assets identified above.[54] Thus, for example, La Scala, the famous Milan opera hall, is an example of the transfer of a government-owned physical facility to a foundation set up to manage it and raise additional support for it. The King Baudouin Foundation in Belgium provides an example of a foundation supported by a stream of revenue coming from a government-owned lottery. Debt swaps that give debtor nations relief from foreign debt in return for their placement of a corresponding amount of local currency into a charitable endowment have occurred in many parts of Latin America and in the case of the Polish-German Cooperation Foundation; and the transformation of non-profit organizations into for-profit firms during which all or a portion of the nonprofit's assets are vested in a charitable foundation has occurred with many nonprofit hospitals and health insurance nonprofits in the US and with nonprofit or cooperative banks in Italy, Austria, and New Zealand.[55]

Not only is this PtP phenomenon important in and of itself, but also it points to a posssible avenue for foundation formation in many less-developed countries.

Not only is this phenomenon important in and of itself, but also it points to a possible avenue for the creation of meaningful charitable endowments in many less-developed countries, where the private wealth to create sizable foundations may be lacking, but where governments are in possession of sizable enterprises or valuable mineral rights whose sale could be used in part to create foundation-type philanthropic endowments dedicated to the health and welfare of local citizens.

Another intriguing development on the frontiers of philanthropy has been the spread of funding collaboratives.

Funding Collaboratives

Another intriguing development on the frontiers of philanthropy has been the spread of funding collaboratives, which offer both individuals and institutions a vehicle for collective grant-making or social-purpose investing. Though they differ significantly in the types of participants they engage (e.g., individuals vs. organizations), the types of resources they jointly assemble or influence (e.g., grants, loans, equity investments), and the types of recipients they support (e.g., individuals, nonprofits, social entrepreneurs, other organizations), these entities share the idea of pooling knowledge and resources, operating collectively, and thereby reducing costs and maximizing impact. They also serve the important social function of bringing like-minded individuals and organizations together around a common purpose.

"Giving circles" constitute one of the most common types of these funding collaboratives. These are groups of people who pool some share of their charitable resources together and decide collectively what organizations to support through grant-making, voluntary assistance, or both. At least 500 such giving circles have been documented in the US, but this probably understates the number of such groups.[56] Some of these are general purpose in orientation, while others are "identity" or "diversity" focused. In addition to their important charitable role, they also perform a social role, bringing together philanthropically inclined individuals in a geographic area and building important social bonds among them.

Similar groupings have now arisen to serve the growing field of social-impact investing. One of these, called TONIIC, has built an exclusive global community of 42 impact investors seeking to place $100 million into global social enterprises. The network shares information about promising ventures among its members, conducts collaborative due diligence reviews, and encourages members to invest in a coordinated fashion in identified, promising ventures.[57]

The collaborative giving and investing bug has not only bitten individuals. It has also smitten organizations, which have come to recognize the need for collective action to address large problems. One of the earliest manifestations of this was the formation of what is now known as Living Cities, which grew out of a collaboration of six foundations determined to halt the deterioration of American cities. Now over 20 years old, this funding collaborative has blossomed into a network of 22 foundations and financial institutions that have collectively invested nearly $1 billion in urban redevelopment projects in 22 US cities.[58] Investors Circle, another example of a funding collaborative, is a 20-year-old network of angel investors, foundations, and family funds that has stimulated the investment of $152 million in some 250 social ventures and funds dedicated to improving the environment, education, health, and community.[59]

A Teeming Subcontinent: Summing Up

In short, an explosion has occurred on the frontiers of philanthropy, a "Big Bang" that has unleashed a host of new actors eager to put their talents and energies into the search for new solutions to age-old problems, and who are finding new resources to finance their efforts. Some of these new actors are mining the supply side of the developing social investment market. Others are providing a variety of support services either to the financiers or to the entities they are generating resources to support. And still others are applying new technologies or new approaches to traditional grant-based philanthropic efforts. Whatever the form, however, the result is a burst of energy and innovation that has not been seen in philanthropic space at least since the time of Andrew Carnegie and John D. Rockefeller, if not quite yet since Jesus, Muhammad, and Maimonides.

Chapter 3

Scouting Philanthropy's
New Frontier II: New Tools

This explosion of new actors has not, of course, taken place in a vacuum. Rather, it has been accompanied, and in some sense prompted, by an enormous proliferation of tools through which to pursue social and environmental objectives. These two developments thus go hand in hand. A revolution is therefore underway not only in the institutional forms functioning in "philanthropic space," broadly conceived, but also in the tools they are deploying to advance philanthropic objectives, supplementing the traditional tool of charitable grants and gifts with a withering array of new financial and nonfinancial instruments.

A withering array of new instruments is now being deployed in the social-purpose arena, many of them for the first time at any scale.

Many of these "new" tools are not new to the world, of course, as noted earlier. Rather, many of them, such as loans, equity investments, bonds, and securitization, have long pedigrees in the world of business finance, and increasingly in government as well.[1] What is new is their deployment in the world of philanthropy and social investment.

What makes these tools increasingly attractive in this new arena is their capacity for *leverage*, for bringing added resources into the social-purpose arena, particularly the kind and scale of resources controlled by banks, investment houses, pension funds, insurance companies, and high-net-worth individuals. A foundation or individual making a grant or gift, for example, typically generates social value equivalent only to the size of the grant or gift. But if that same foundation or individual uses its resources to guarantee a loan made by a commercial bank or pension fund it can leverage far more resources than it puts at risk.

While many of the new tools being introduced into social-purpose activity are not new to the world, their deployment in this new arena has necessitated a variety of adjustments and modifications, many of them highly innovative if not yet fully legitimized or understood. Loans have therefore had to be supplemented with a variety of "credit enhancements" to induce risk-averse private investors to keep interest rates low enough for social-purpose organizations to afford. Equity investments have had to be modified to get around legal prohibitions on nonprofit distribution of profits. And new types of bonds have had to be invented to get around cumbersome "rating" provisions and ensure a flow of long-term, patient capital into promising social ventures.

While a full elaboration of the evolving shape of these new tools is the task for the chapters in our companion book, *New Frontiers of Philanthropy*, a brief overview of some of the central features of the major tools may help prepare readers for the fuller explications available in this more extensive volume. As before, we differentiate between the relatively new *financial investment* tools, such as loans and equities, and other, *nonfinancial*, tools that make new use of interventions such as crowd sourcing or socially responsible investing and purchasing.

Social-Impact Financial Investment Tools

Loans are by far the most common social-impact investment tool.

Loans

A useful starting point for the discussion of financial investment instruments is the tool of loans, or debt, and its next of kin, "credit enhancements." Loans are by far the most common social-impact investment tool. When the US Congress opened the door for US foundations to make so-called "program-related investments" in the Tax Reform Act of 1969 and to count them as part of foundations' required "payout requirement," it mostly had loans in mind. And not surprisingly, loans have remained the dominant form of PRIs, accounting in 2006–2007, the latest period for which data are available, for nearly 80 percent of all PRI transactions and over 85 percent of all PRI dollars.[2] Cooch and Kramer found a similar picture when they broadened the lens from PRIs to

Table 3.1
Asset classes of social-impact investments

Instrument type	Number	%	Amount (USD, m)	%
Private debt	1,345	61%	2,296	52%
Bilateral loan agreement	152	7%	191	4%
Deposit	106	5%	70	2%
Guarantee	10	0%	73	2%
Equity-like debt	48	2%	78	2%
Public debt	1	0%	2	0%
Subtotal, debt[a]	**1,662**	**75%**	**2,710**	**62%**
Private equity	548	25%	1,655	38%
Public equity	2	0%	10	0%
Subtotal, equity[a]	**550**	**25%**	**1,665**	**38%**
Real assets (reported)	**1**	**0%**	**2**	**0%**
Total	**2,213**	**100%**	**4,377**	**100**

Source: Jasmin Saltuk, Amit Bouri, and Giselle Leung, *Insight into the Impact Investment Market: An In-Depth Analysis of Investor Perspectives and over 2,200 Transactions* (London: J.P. Morgan Social Investment, 2011), 6.
[a] Debt and equity are sums of the rows above, respectively.

"mission investing" by US foundations more generally: of 520 such investments identified, 63 percent were loans and another 19 percent some other type of debt.[3] This picture has been further confirmed by an even broader, global study of 2,213 social-impact investments made by a pool of 52 investors. As shown in Table 3.1, as of 2011 these social-impact investors had $4.4 billion in social-impact investments outstanding, of which 75 percent of the deals and 62 percent of the assets ($2.7 billion in all) took the form of various types of debt.[4]

Loans are one form of *debt*. The basic concept of a loan is fairly straightforward: a lender provides cash (the principal) to a borrower, who is obligated to repay the cash, typically with interest, either over time or at an agreed-upon time in the future (the maturity date). Compared to other forms of debt, such as bonds (discussed below), loans tend to be smaller in size and shorter in maturity. But all forms of debt differ from the other major type of investment capital, *equity*, which involves a share of ownership and does not create an obligation for repayment unless the recipient entity earns a profit. Loans thus entail less risk than equities, but correspondingly typically involve less return.

As loans have come to be used in the social-impact arena, however, they have grown in complexity.[5] Loans can thus be "secured," that is, backed up by some asset that the lender can seize if the loan is not repaid, or "unsecured." Real estate loans have therefore traditionally been the least risky because they are backed by tangible property. Social ventures frequently have little tangible property, however, which means that they are rarely in a position to offer security for their loans. J.P. Morgan's 2011 study of 2,213 social-impact investments cited earlier thus found that 60 percent of the debt investments were unsecured. Loans can also be "senior," or "subordinated." A senior loan has the first call on any payment or assets in case a borrower is unable to pay its loan obligations, whereas a subordinated loan is paid off only after other lenders or investors. For-profit providers of loans to social ventures tend to require a senior position to reduce their risk. Finally, loans can be "soft" or "hard." Soft loans are ones that offer flexible or lenient terms for repayment, usually at lower than market interest rates. Such flexible terms are typically needed by start-ups and even second-stage social ventures due to their frequent lack of tangible assets with which to secure their loans and the uncertain prospects for their enterprises.

Credit enhancements are designed to alter the risk-return ratio sufficiently to allow private investors to participate.

Credit Enhancements

Due to the relative riskiness of many social ventures, a variety of inducements have had to be added to loans in order to attract lenders and get them to accept the below-market rates that early-stage social ventures typically require. This was the case with the African Agricultural Capital Fund (AACP) deal cited at the outset of this book. In order to induce J.P. Morgan's Social Finance Unit to make an $8 million loan to this fund, the US Agency for International Development had to guarantee the loan, thus protecting J.P. Morgan against any loss.[6] Such guarantees are one type of inducements known as "credit enhancements." Credit enhancements are designed to alter the risk-return ratio sufficiently to allow private investors to get around their legal obligation to maximize profit for their shareholders enough to participate in a social-purpose deal. In other cases, foundations or other social investors with a "social-impact first" orientation will provide grants, subordinated loans, or equity capital as the base of a funding "stack" to absorb any initial losses on an investment. In this way they protect private investors who hold more senior positions in an investment consortium, thereby encouraging the private investors to participate and lowering their return requirements. Thus, in one recent deal, Fair Finance, a UK microfinance lender, generated a £2 million loan from Société Générale and BNP Paribas that was underwritten by a £750,000 foundation grant and a £350,000 soft loan from Big Society Capital, the UK Government's social investment fund.[7]

Fixed-income securities

Another class of debt instruments increasingly being used in the social-impact investing arena consists of *fixed-income securities*. These are essentially huge loans with longer maturities, typically sold through underwriters or investment banks that then market them to various types of investors, including pension funds, insurance companies, and high net worth individuals. Given their size and highly indirect marketing, fixed-income securities are usually put through an elaborate *rating process* before they are offered to the investing public. Fixed-income financing is an enormous component of global capital markets with an estimated $95 trillion of outstanding debt at the end of 2010 despite the recent financial meltdown. They therefore have the capability to generate huge sums of capital for major undertakings.[8]

The most common type of fixed-income security is a long-term *bond*, but shorter term *notes* are also used.[9] Borrowers who raise funds through fixed-income securities enter into contracts to pay bondholders the amount borrowed on an agreed maturity date and to pay interest, known as the *coupon*, at regular intervals over the life of the bond. Bondholders, in turn, can sell the bonds to other investors if they choose to do so, with the price varying depending on the relation between the *coupon rate* on the bond and prevailing interest rates in the market.

Given their scale and complexity, fixed-income securities are used most commonly by fairly mature institutions with reliable streams of revenue capable of covering coupon payments. Among social-purpose organizations, universities and hospitals have been the heaviest users of fixed-income securities, often with the aid, in the US, of a credit enhancement in the form of tax deductions for investors on the coupon payments they receive.

Especially imaginative has been the Community Investment (CI) Note mechanism launched in 1995 by the Calvert Foundation.

But innovative ways have been found to tap this lucrative tool to finance other social-purpose activities as well. At one end of the continuum of innovations is the International Finance Facility for Immunization (IFFIm), an ambitious global effort to underwrite the production, distribution, and delivery of vaccines against polio, measles, tetanus, and other deadly diseases to 500 million children in 70 of the world's poorest countries. The financing of this effort has been pursued through bonds, but bonds that will ultimately be paid for through guarantees provided by several European governments and marketed by Goldman Sachs and Deutsche Bank. As the IFFIm website explains, "by issuing bonds in the capital markets" IFFIm "converts long-term government pledges into immediately available cash resources." The inaugural issue of IFFIm bonds in 2006 raised $1.7 billion, 1.7 times the original $1 billion goal, and $3.6 billion have so far been raised in toto.[10]

Equally imaginative has been the Community Investment (CI) Note mechanism launched in 1995 by the Calvert Social Investment Foundation (Calvert Foundation), a Community Development Finance Institution headquartered in the US, with support from the Ford, MacArthur, and Mott foundations. CI Notes are essentially minibonds, unrated, and sold directly to individual investors by the Calvert Foundation, indirectly by brokers, and now online through a subsidiary of eBay. Investors can choose the term (1, 3, 5, 7, or 10 years) and the interest rate they would like to receive (0, 1, 2, or 3 percent). Calvert Foundation then invests the proceeds either in community-based intermediaries promoting affordable housing or inner-city development in the US, or microfinance and fair-trade farmworker cooperatives internationally. To date, this innovative fixed-income instrument has generated $220 million of capital from 10,000 citizen-investors with losses below 1 percent—all of it offset by Calvert Foundation reserves—thus ensuring timely payment of principal and interest to all investors.[11] Perhaps equally importantly, the Calvert experience has led a number of other social-purpose CDFIs and related institutions to launch their own unsecured and unrated retail note programs to raise capital for social-purpose initiatives.

Other examples of credit enhancements attached to bonds include the $30 million bond protection provided by the Bill and Melinda Gates Foundation that allowed KIPP Houston, a for-profit network of charter schools, to raise up to $300 million in tax-exempt bond proceeds from private investors for the expansion of its charter schools network at no cost to the Gates Foundation. More generally, the US Treasury created a new CDFI Bond Guarantee Program in 2011 to assist CDFIs to finance their affordable housing and community development activities in the wake of the 2008 financial crisis.

Securitization

Closely related to the tool of bonds is an additional debt-related instrument known as *securitization*. Securitization is the mechanism that "secondary market" actors use to bundle individual mortgages or other debt instruments together for sale to investors in order to generate capital that primary lenders can use to make new loans. Like many of the other "new" tools entering the arena of social-purpose finance, securitization has long been used in the standard financial arena. Indeed, it was problems in the mainline securitization field that produced the US financial crisis in 2008, as securitized mortgages turned out to be worth far less than advertised to unwitting investors, including some of the country's premier banks and investment houses. But securitization has entered the world of social-purpose finance as well, although the global financial crisis has put a chill on investor willingness to buy the securities backed by social-purpose loans even though these loans have performed much better than the ones issued by mainline for-profit lenders.

Securitization involves the assembly of hundreds or thousands of individual loans into packages for sale to so-called special purpose entities, which then issue bonds or other securities backed by the loans for sale to ultimate investors.[12] The loans securing the bonds can be home mortgages (mortgage-backed securities) or loans for various other purposes, such as car loans, credit card balances, or, in the social-purpose arena, loans to microenterprises or charter schools (asset-backed securities). The transactions involved in setting prices for the securities backed by these bundles of loans are naturally highly complex since estimates must be made of the riskiness and likely returns on the underlying loans given their maturities, interest rates, likelihood of being paid off, and the relation of all of this to general market conditions.

Given the uncertainties traditionally surrounding social-purpose investment, securitization made relatively slow progress in this field until relatively recently. Instead, secondary market actors in this investment arena had to rely on private placements and the creation of specially organized funding consortia rather than the established machinery available to market "rated" securities. In addition, they have had to secure various credit enhancements such as bond guarantees, and reserves against losses, from angel investors or philanthropic institutions.

In the early 2000s, however, secondary market operators in the housing and microfinance arenas finally succeeded in penetrating this highly lucrative vehicle for channeling significant resources into social-purpose activity. In particular, in 2004 the Community Reinvestment Fund (CRF), a US-based secondary market focusing on low-income housing and community development mortgages, managed to assemble and market the first "rated" bond backed by low-income housing and community development loans, allowing it to attract funds in the process from eight new institutional investors whose strict investing guidelines would have kept it out of the deal without the rating. CRF subsequently brought three other rated securitizations to market before the 2008 financial crisis cooled investor responses.

The global microfinance industry has also managed to find its way to the securitization tool. Blue Orchard, a Swiss microfinance investment fund, brought the first microfinance security to market in 2004 and managed to raise $67 million, which was used to refresh the capital of microfinance investment intermediaries (MIIs) across the globe. Subsequently, at least nine other securitization deals for microfinance loans have been successfully closed, the most recent being the huge $180 million securitization successfully marketed by the Bangladesh Rural Advancement Committee (BRAC) in 2006. As of 2008, a total of $525 million had been raised through the securitization of microfinance loans globally, a sizable sum, though still only 12 percent of all outstanding MII investments.

Even more attractive to social-purpose organizations than securitization is the tool of equity investments.

Equity

Even more attractive to social-purpose organizations than securitization is the tool of equity investments. The loans that underlie securitizations must ultimately be paid back with interest, after all. Equity investments carry no such obligation. Equity investment usually takes the form of selling ownership shares in an enterprise to an equity investor in exchange for capital. Unlike with debt, the organization has no legal obligation to repay the amount invested or to pay interest. Equity investors usually invest in organizations that they believe will grow. In return they expect to receive dividends paid out of the organization's earnings and/or capital gain on the sale of the organization or on selling their shares to other investors. But if the enterprise does not pay dividends or does not do well, the equity investor can lose his or her money. Equity investments thus carry the highest risk and therefore typically command the highest returns.

Equity finance has historically been less commonly used by social-purpose organizations, but recent developments are changing this.

Equity finance has historically been less commonly used than debt finance by social-purpose organizations.[13] One reason for the historically limited use is that many social-purpose organizations are nonprofit in form and are legally prohibited from issuing ownership shares or distributing any profits they may earn. What is more, even for-profit social enterprises take considerable time to generate profits, making them unattractive to social-purpose investors. Even patient capital providers like foundations have been somewhat reluctant to make equity investments. Thus, the 2007 study of 52 US foundation mission investors by Cooch and Kramer found that only 14 percent of the 520 investments made by these institutions were equity investments. Although equities accounted for 45 percent of the investment dollars, moreover, the overwhelming majority of these were real estate deals where a tangible asset was involved.[14] More generally, a J.P. Morgan study of 52 social-impact investment funds with at least $25 million in assets under management found in 2011 that equity investments accounted for only 25 percent of the 2,213 investments identified, though they accounted for 38 percent of the assets.[15]

Nevertheless, the recent growth of social enterprises, many of which take the form of for-profits, cooperatives, or other hybrid forms, has opened the social-purpose field to a much more substantial use of equities and to the growth of a wide assortment of equity funds to provide them. Perhaps reflecting this, a more recent J.P. Morgan survey suggests some expansion in social-impact investor use of equity. According to this survey, over 80 percent of a sample of social-impact investors reported making some use of equity investments in 2012 compared to only 66 percent that reported using private debt instruments, though this recent study did not report the share of deals or finances that involved the equity tool.[16]

Much of this social-purpose equity investment takes the form of so-called private equity, that is, investments in firms that are not listed on regulated stock exchanges open to the public. Rather, the investments are handled privately, typically through equity *funds*, which have grown substantially in both numbers and assets in recent years. One estimate of the private equity fund market in the US identifies 375 so-called socially responsible "alternative investment funds," that is, funds that invest in unlisted companies that incorporate environmental, social, and governance (ESG) criteria into their investment decisions. Taken together, these funds have close to $81 billion of assets under management, an increase of nearly 16 percent over the previous year. Of this total, roughly $34 billion are in private equity and venture capital funds and $44 billion in real estate funds, some portion of which also takes the form of equity investments.[17]

The Community Development Venture Capital Alliance (CDVCA), the trade association supporting one branch of this industry that focuses on supporting business development in lagging regions, describes its members' purpose as being to "provide equity capital to businesses in underinvested markets, seeking market-rate financial returns as well as the creation of good jobs, wealth, and entrepreneurial capacity."[18] Kentucky Highlands, one of the earliest of these funds, was originally formed in 1968 to stimulate growth and create employment opportunities in an economically depressed nine-county region of southeastern Kentucky but has since expanded its geographic focus and leveraged its original funding from the federal government by attracting bank capital stimulated by the Community Reinvestment Act. In 35 years, Kentucky Highlands's equity investments have helped 220 businesses generate $178 million in support, creating more than 9,900 jobs and generating risk-adjusted market rates of returns to its investors.[19]

Equity finance through equity funds is hardly restricted to the US and other developed markets, however. A considerable number of such funds have found it possible to undertake equity funding with meaningful returns in emerging markets as well. Thus, for-profit firms such as UK-based Bridges Ventures, Dubai-based Willow Impact Investors, and

> ## Box 3.1
> ## Aavishkaar International
>
> *"We at Aavishkaar have taken it upon ourselves to be the leaders of micro equity investments to create scalable small entrepreneurs with significant social impact."*
>
> "[The] Aavishkaar I [Fund] was created to promote inclusive development in rural and semi-urban regions in India. The fund's mission was based on the premise that promising Micro, Small to Medium-sized enterprises (MSMEs) will help drive positive changes in the underserved regions of the country...Aavishkaar I's capital [US$14 million] is fully deployed in 22 companies... operating across Agriculture, Dairy, Healthcare, Water and Sanitation, Technology for Development, Education and Renewable Energy sectors.
>
> *Source*: Aavishkaar International, http://www.aavishkaar.in.

Singapore-based Aavishkaar International have established operations adhering fairly closely to a classical private equity model, raising money from investors expecting a market rate of return and finding promising ventures serving the "bottom of the pyramid" in which to invest (see Box 3.1).[20]

In addition to the private equity reaching ventures through equity funds, individual investors also make considerable amounts of equity investment in social-purpose ventures directly, often with the aid of angel investor or social entrepreneurial networks such as the Social Venture Network, Investors' Circle, the Slow Money Alliance, or TONIIC. Investors' Circle, for example, is a network of 150 investors, donors, and family offices that has helped to place $150 million of investment in over 200 separate companies and networks addressing social and environmental objectives.[21]

Private equity can take a variety of forms. "Standard equity" is typically used for more mature firms needing equity to scale up proven operations. Another type of equity, known as "quasi equity," discussed below, is more often used for early-stage firms needing greater leeway or for nonprofit social enterprises that are barred from sharing ownership with investors or distributing profits to owners and therefore not able to use standard equity. Even standard equity takes a variety of forms, moreover, such as "common stock," "preferred stock," and "convertible preferred equity." These forms of so-called standard equity offer investors successively expanded ownership rights and privileged access to any gains that the firm may generate. The greater the uncertainties surrounding the enterprise, the more such rights and privileges will be demanded by equity investors.

Because equity provides no guarantee of return, equity investors, particularly private equity investors, that is, those investing in companies not listed on any public exchange, typically take great care in assessing enterprise capabilities and pinning down their rights to review enterprise decisions, often taking positions on enterprise boards. Complex "term sheets" are utilized to detail such things as the amounts and uses of the equity funds invested, the valuation of the firm and its business model, the exact type of equity instrument being used, the decision rights granted to the investor, and incentives or controls placed on the owners or managers.[22]

Beyond the capital promoting social-purpose activities through *private* equity funding, which typically focuses on early-stage or mezzanine finance, another type of social-purpose equity investment has also grown enormously in recent years as a byproduct of the emergence of investment screening mechanisms such as the UN Principles for Responsible Investment (UNPRI). These mechanisms apply socially and environmentally conscious investment criteria to *public* equity being sought by more mature firms through regulated stock exchanges.[23] Some 230 pension funds and other investment institutions controlling over $25 trillion in assets have endorsed the UNPRI criteria. As of 2011, $3.3 trillion in investment assets were being managed under some form of responsible investment criteria in the US, and the comparable figure in Europe as of 2011 was €6.8 trillion (close to US$9 trillion at 2012 exchange rates), with approximately one-third of these assets in Europe in equities.[24]

Quasi Equity

Powerful as equity finance is as a source of capital, it is not universally available for social-purpose activities. For one thing, many social enterprises are quite young. A survey of social enterprises conducted in the UK in 2011, for example, revealed that 54 percent of social enterprises were less than 10 years old, and 31 percent less than five years old. By comparison, the comparable percentages for all small businesses in the UK were 33 percent and 15 percent.[25] Given the amount of time it takes for an enterprise to become reliably profitable, this can deter equity investors. In addition, many social enterprises are nonprofit in legal form and are barred from issuing ownership shares to potential investors or distributing profits to them in the form of dividends. Finally, even where they are investing in for-profit firms, equity investors can worry about whether they will be able to find a market for their shares if they want to exit from an equity investment in a social venture.

Quasi equity essentially gives investors returns that look like equity returns but without giving them ownership shares in the organization.

At the same time, all of these social-purpose ventures are in need of risk capital both to get started and to expand, and loans may not be appropriate if returns are not secure enough to meet loan repayments. Fortunately, a number of innovations have surfaced to cope with this challenge. One of these is the creation of "matched bargain markets" or full-fledged *social stock exchanges* as detailed above. Such exchanges provide a reasonably reliable market through which investors can exit from social-purpose equity investments without costly transaction costs.[26] Another innovation is the use of structured finance instruments that pool different types of finance in a single deal, with equity investors buffered by other sources that provide grant funding or loans to absorb the initial risk of loss. Aavishkaar International, for example, reports that its investment instruments are generally "a mix of common equity and convertible debentures. When appropriate, we also use quasi equity, preferred convertibles, preferred redeemable, mezzanine loans, royalties and other venture capital instruments. Flexibility in structuring of investments to help scale

businesses while minimizing promoter's dilution is one of
our major differentiators."[27]

One of the more interesting developments in the field of
social-purpose equity investing, however, is the expanded use
of various forms of so-called quasi equity. Quasi equity essentially gives investors returns that look like equity returns but
without giving them ownership shares in the organization
(see Box 3.2). This is done by creating some form of debt con-
tract or royalty arrangement that guarantees investors a share
of revenue growth either for the organization as a whole or
a particular program.[28] For example, HCT Group, a network
of UK charities that provide transportation services for disadvantaged communities but also compete for commercial
transportation contracts, used a quasi-equity instrument to
generate £4 million (US$6.4 million at 2012 exchange rates)
to purchase vehicles and facilities, but did so without diluting
the nonprofit ownership structure of the organization.[29]

Box 3.2
Quasi-Equity

"Sometimes debt financing is inappropriate for social
sector organisations, especially in the high-risk start-up
phase. Equally, equity investment may not be possible
if the organisation is not structured to issue shares.

"A quasi-equity investment allows an investor to
benefit from the future revenues of an organisation
through a royalty payment which is a fixed percentage
of income. However the investor may gain nothing if
the organisation does not perform. This is similar to a
conventional equity investment, but does not require
an organisation to issue shares. The share of future
revenues that a quasi-equity investor receives is usually linked to income and not profit, as social sector
organisations are often not structured to make profits
for distribution."

Source: "What is social Investment," Big Society Capital,
accessed June 12, 2013, http://www.bigsocietycapital.com/
what-social-investment.

...monetizing the future savings to government from promising preventive services and using them to...to attract private investors.

Social-Impact Bonds

Another innovative tool that has recently made its appearance in the social-purpose finance arena goes variously by the name of *social-impact bonds* or, in the US, *pay-for-success*. Social-impact bonds provide a way to finance preventive services that can ultimately save governments or other entities substantial sums over the long run but that typically have trouble attracting the upfront capital needed to sustain themselves until such savings materialize. They do so by monetizing the future savings to government from promising preventive services and using them, or at least the promise of them, to attract private investors willing to take the risk of financing the services upfront in return for a guaranteed share of the savings once evidence of success begins to be demonstrated.

Here's how they work: governments recruit intermediaries who believe they know how to structure a preventative human-service initiative that can save the governments money once put in place, and who are willing to recruit private-sector funders who will cover the multiyear upfront cost. In return, the government pledges that if the intervention meets or exceeds its goals, the government will return the investors' original investment plus some return based on a sliding scale dependent on the degree of success the intervention achieves.

As this suggests, social-impact bonds (SIBs) are really not bonds in the true sense of the word, but rather, like quasi equity, a strange amalgam of equity and debt. Like equity, social-impact bonds only generate returns for their investors if the activities they support meet certain performance thresholds. If not, investors are at risk of losing their principal or ending up with no net return on their investment. Like bonds, however, SIBs have fixed terms and the upside return is capped.[30]

The initial trial of this new tool is underway at Peterborough Prison in the UK. A British social investment fund called Social Finance raised £5 million (≈US$ 8 million) from 17 investors to fund a comprehensive rehabilitation program for first-time offenders leaving the Peterborough facility over a six-year period, with a promise from the UK government that it will pay back this investment with interest on a sliding scale if the intervention achieves a target reduction in the recidivism rate of the affected offenders compared to a control group.[31]

Already this idea has spread to the US, where it goes by the name "pay-for-success." The first US adoption was announced in early August 2012 in New York City with a similar first-offender focus, but with capital advanced not mostly by charitable foundations, as in the UK example, but by the for-profit investment firm, Goldman Sachs, which is investing $9.6 million in loan funds in the effort.[32]

Other New Tools

In addition to the social-impact investing tools newly available on the frontiers of philanthropy are a variety of other new instruments or approaches being deployed in the social and environmental action arena. Three of these in particular also deserve attention here: microinsurance, socially responsible investing and purchasing, and new types of grants.

Recent estimates put the share of low-income people with insurance in the world's 100 poorest countries at less than 3 percent.

Microinsurance

Less exotic, but no less powerful, a new tool of philanthropy is microinsurance. Like many of the other new tools examined previously, there is nothing especially new about the tool of insurance. What is new is the creation of adaptations of the standard tool of insurance to make it accessible to the millions of people living almost totally exposed to multiple forms of risk at the bottom of the economic pyramid. Recent estimates put the share of low-income people with insurance in the world's 100 poorest countries at less than 3 percent.[33] This means that over 97 percent of the populations in these countries remain exposed to any of a series of typical threats to their security—illness, drought, storms, floods, or death of a family member—that can drive them further into poverty or frustrate efforts to escape from it.

While many savings or insurance schemes, such as funeral insurance, have surfaced indigenously to help mitigate this exposure, these typically lack the crucial feature required for cost-effective and reliable insurance—namely, risk-pooling over a large enough group of people to reduce premiums to a low enough level to be affordable while providing enough protection to be worth the cost.

Fortunately, however, thanks to cooperation among national governments, international organizations such as the International Labour Organization, and private insurance companies, new "microinsurance" products have surfaced and begun to tap the bottom-of-the-pyramid market.[34] One estimate in 2010 put the number of people covered by microinsurance schemes globally at 135 million. But this just scratches the surface of the global need and is heavily concentrated in only a few countries. Indeed, a 2010 Swiss Re study estimates the number of people living on $1.25 to $4.00 a day who could afford small premiums but are not covered by conventional insurance to be in the neighborhood of 2.6 billion, with an additional 1.4 billion people living on less than $1.25 a day potentially reachable with the help of subsidies.[35]

As with so many other of the new tools being deployed on the frontiers of philanthropy, the limited penetration of insurance products into the bottom-of-the-pyramid market is a consequence of the delayed recognition on the part of for-profit insurance providers of the possibilities for profitable operations that this market offered. Also at work, however, have been the inherent complexities of the insurance product—the product must be marketed to huge numbers of people in order to be viable, mechanisms must be put in place to verify the occurrence of an insured loss and calculate its value, some way must be found to estimate the likelihood of such losses in advance so that premiums can be calculated, and the premiums must be kept low enough to be affordable by low-income clients.

Overcoming these barriers has required considerable innovation and teamwork on the part of governments, insurers, foundations, international organizations, and other actors with connections to those on the bottom of the pyramid. The innovations underway are already striking: a program in India that has mobilized private insurance companies to extend health insurance to some 63 million individuals living below the poverty line in 25 Indian states;[36] claim verification systems for crop insurance that index payments to weather conditions and for livestock that use radio-frequency identification devices; mobilization of microinsurance finance institutions, such as Prodem in Bolivia, or utility companies, such as CODENSA in Colombia, with significant links to the low-income populations of their countries, to market a variety of insurance products to their under-served customers. These innovations have been encouraged, and in turn disseminated, through a growing network of infrastructure organizations such as the Microinsurance Network, the ILO facility mentioned earlier, the Joint Learning Network for Universal Coverage, and the Munich Climate Insurance Initiative.[37]

Socially Responsible Investing and Purchasing

A rather different mechanism for achieving social and environmental purposes without the need of complex financial instruments takes the form of *socially responsible investing and purchasing*. Advocates of social impact investing have been somewhat dismissive of this route to social and environmental change, seeing it chiefly as a way to "minimize negative impact rather than proactively create positive social or environmental benefit."[38] But, in practice, this mechanism has gained considerable traction on the positive side of the ledger as well.

The scale of assets in Europe managed according to a...socially responsible investment standard as of 2012 [stood at] €6.8 trillion, or close to US$9 trillion.

The key to socially responsible investing and purchasing is the mobilization of investors and consumers to pressure companies to operate in socially and environmentally responsible ways. This can be done through a variety of channels—promoting positive or negative investment *screens*, establishing investment *standards, voting shares* of stock in ways that encourage responsible corporate behavior, introducing *resolutions* for vote by shareholders, engaging corporate leaders in *dialogue, boycotting* undesirable products, or encouraging purchase of other products that meet various criteria, such as those relating to labor rights, health concerns, treatment of animals, sustainable forestry, or support for indigenous people.[39]

Though hardly entirely new, socially responsible investment and purchasing expanded considerably in the 1990s and into the 2000s, as new technologies and increased corporate sensitivity to risks to their "reputational capital" gave added leverage to investors and consumers with social concerns on their minds. One important boost was the development in 2006 of the UN Principles of Responsible Investment, which established standards for responsible environmental, social, and governance behavior on the part of corporations. By 2012, as noted earlier, some 230 pension funds and other investment funds had endorsed these principles and pledged to follow them in their own investment activities.

Socially responsible investment has attracted particular interest in European investment circles. The European Sustainable Investment Forum (Eurosif), a network of 79 pension and investment funds and eight national affiliated SIFs, puts the scale of assets in Europe managed according to one or another type of socially responsible investment standard as of 2012 at €6.8 trillion, or close to US$9 trillion.[40] What is more, the growth of socially responsible investing appears to have outpaced the growth of overall investment on the continent in recent years, with four out of six responsible investment strategies growing by more than 35 percent per annum since 2009.[41] In the US, the comparable figure is a sizable $3.3 trillion of assets managed under responsible investing guidelines.

Whether because of such socially responsible investment pressures or other factors, socially responsible investment reporting has become a staple of larger corporations globally. Institutions such as Instituto Ethos in Brazil have actively diffused this practice in their countries and regions, with over 600 firms in Brazil alone producing social responsibility reports showing their alignment with Ethos's demanding standards. As one observer put it: Ethos "officialized" corporate social responsibility (CSR) in Brazil, making it "the thing to do for corporations that wanted to be considered progressive and responsive to the country's enormous social problems."[42]

Side by side with the expansion of ethical investing has been an expansion of ethical purchasing. As Lydenberg and Grace report, the global market for organic food and beverages already totaled $23 billion as of 2007, and organic personal care sales in the US alone totaled another $9 billion. As pressures mount on businesses to report on their social responsibility practices, they have joined consumers as socially responsible purchasers, utilizing their supply chain management to serve their social responsibility aspirations. Japanese, European, and some Latin American companies have been especially active in this fashion, as have their governments.

To be sure, while the growth of socially responsible investing and purchasing have been impressive, they still represent a tiny fraction of the activity in their respective domains. What is more, the evidence of actual financial impact of either tactic on the financial health or stock prices of companies remains scant.[43] Nevertheless, there is evidence that at least some companies are behaving as if it does make a difference, which may be all that counts.

Some important innovations have also recently appeared in the grant world as well.

Grants

While much of the buzz on the new frontiers of philanthropy has focused on non-grant forms of assistance on grounds that traditional grant-making is not capable of achieving significant leverage, in fact some important innovations have also recently appeared in the grant world as well. What is more, these innovations come on top of a variety of prior ways in which grant-making has attempted to achieve greater leverage through such devices as start-up grants, matching grants, and pilot projects intended to demonstrate workable innovations that governments can subsequently take up.

One such recent innovation is the practice of "venture philanthropy" covered previously in this volume, which combines big-bet grant-making with intensive organizational capacity-building and close-in supervision. But another whole area of innovation involves various forms of competition pursued through prizes and crowd sourcing. This form of grant-making has been described as "a breath of fresh air in the world of grants."[44] Unlike traditional grants, which are essentially designed and managed by foundation program officers, competitions, prizes, and crowd sourcing begin from the premise that there is a market of ideas and that the best use of foundation resources is to tap into it as broadly as possible.

Unlike traditional grants, prizes and crowd sourcing tap into the existing market of ideas.

Some prizes are used after the fact to reward notable accomplishments in a field. Examples here include the Pulitzer Prizes for literature or the Nobel Prize. Increasingly, however, a different type of prize is emerging that takes the form of an open competition to provide a solution to a concrete problem. Examples here include the X Prize, which offers $10 million to the first team to achieve a specific goal, such as designing a private vehicle that could fly a pilot to the edge of outer space; or the Case Foundation's Make It Your Own Awards, which allow citizens to vote on which of a number of community improvement organizations Case should reward with a $25,000 grant; or Toyota's Ideas for Good prize, which it gives to the person or organization that applies one of five categories of automotive technology developed by Toyota successfully in another field to solve a community or public problem.

According to a recent McKinsey and Company report, such prizes have mushroomed in recent decades. Almost $250 million in new prize money became available during the first decade of the twenty-first century, and the total funds available through large prizes more than tripled over the decade of the 2000s, surpassing $375 million. Indeed, McKinsey and Company estimates that the total prize sector could now be worth as much as $1 to $2 billion.[45]

Conclusion

In short, an enormous explosion is taking place in both the actors and the tools occupying the new frontiers of philanthropy. But how can we explain this phenomenon, and what insights can such explanations offer into the durability of this phenomenon? It is to these more analytical questions that we must now turn.

Chapter 4

Why Now?

From the evidence at hand, it appears that a number of underlying forces have been at work to produce the new frontiers of philanthropy at the present time. What is more, both demand and supply factors have been at work.

The Demand Side of the New Social Capital Market

That a new frontier has formed in the world of philanthropy and social investment in recent years seems due, in the first instance, to a set of demand factors that have gained salience during this period. These factors take at least three different forms.

The New Inferno

In the first place, long-standing problems of poverty and inequality that continue to entrap large swaths of the world's population have recently been joined by serious environmental threats to form a modern version of Dante's inferno, with its multiple circles of human suffering. Today's counterpart to Virgil, Dante's guide through the nine circles of hell, is the environmentalist Lester Brown, whose *World on the Edge* paints as vivid a picture as did Dante's *Divine Comedy* of what awaits us if bad habits and current tendencies continue unabated.[1]

A gathering perfect storm of trends threatens our civilization.

As Brown puts it: "A gathering 'perfect storm' of trends threatens to send civilization into economic and political chaos."[2] To Dante's imagined nine circles of hell Brown adds six terrifying trends.

First up in the catalog of sins from which our world is suffering in Brown's account is the depletion of the earth's water supply as a consequence of overdrilling by farmers and deforestation of large portions of the earth's land area. As a consequence, water tables are falling and wells going dry in some 20 countries, including the three that produce half of the world's grain—China, India, and the US.

Water shortage, in turn, combines with overfarming, over-grazing, and expanding urbanization to yield the second dev-astating trend: loss of the earth's topsoil and ultimately of its inherent productivity, leading ultimately to desertification, when the earth becomes unable to support life. Desertification now affects 25 percent of the earth's land area and threatens the livelihood of more than 1 billion people, with two huge dust bowls forming in the Asian heartland and in central Africa, and with evidence of severe drought even in the American West.

Desertification now affects 25 percent of the earth's land area and threatens the livelihood of more than 1 billion people.

These problems are in turn intensified by the third devastat-ing trend: overconsumption of fossil fuels and the resulting warming of the earth, posing enormous threats to the food supply, generating more severe and more numerous weather emergencies, and displacing millions of people.

Those displaced by the rising seas, more destructive storms, and expanding deserts will then become part of a fourth devastating trend: a massive growth in the numbers of "environmental refugees," people forced from their homes by the devastating storms provoked by rising temperatures, by the advancing desert, by falling water tables, and by unregu-lated toxic wastes. This phenomenon is, in turn, being accen-tuated by a fifth distressing trend: rapid population growth, especially in the least prosperous regions of the world. This has produced what Brown terms a "demographic trap," as larger families produce poverty and poverty leads to larger families. At least 40 percent of the population in the world's 20 poorest countries are thus under 15. Large numbers of youngsters, especially young men, without decent employ-ment opportunities, in turn becomes a prescription for disaf-fection, crime, and ultimately even insurgencies.

All of this is contributing to the sixth deadly sin: a striking rise in the number of failed states. And as states fail, further deterioration of the economic infrastructure of roads, power, water, and sanitation systems ensues, inviting further frag-mentation of authority and the rise of rival armed gangs and cliques. Somalia, Chad, Sudan, the Congo, Afghanistan, and

Iraq have moved fairly far down this road, and even highly populated countries like Pakistan and Nigeria have significant portions of their territories in "failed state" status.

Taken together, this complex of miseries has massively expanded the need for serious attention to poverty alleviation and long-term solutions to food, water, health, and environmental crises—not alone to relieve human suffering in the places where it is concentrated, but to avoid terrifying consequences for all peoples in all places.

Tapped-out Governmental and Charitable Resources

These interrelated environmental, economic, social, and political needs would be difficult to meet under any circumstances. But they are being confronted now by a world that has been experiencing enormous economic shocks, unsustainable governmental spending, and charitable resources that, while growing, do not come close to being able to deliver the resources needed to address the problems that exist. With the US debt now 107 percent of the country's gross domestic profit, and debt levels in France and Germany above the European Union's legislated upper limit of 60 percent of GDP, even the world's richest countries are in no position to take robust action to mitigate these global problems.[3] Indeed, most of them are in cutback mode with respect to some of the most crucial social and environmental protections for their own people, and this in the face of still escalating unemployment in many places.[4] And global charity, even generously estimated, is a very small fraction of what governments are able to spend. Even in the US, philanthropy from all sources—individuals, foundations, and corporations—accounts for no more than 10 percent of the income of the country's nonprofit organizations, and a dramatically smaller share of overall government social welfare spending.[5]

The Rise of Social Entrepreneurs

A third set of demand factors that has contributed enormously to the developments outlined here has been the appearance of a new social force in the form of a growing army of so-called social entrepreneurs, "restless people," as journalist David Bornstein has styled them, who become almost possessed by imaginative new ideas to address major problems and who are "so relentless in the pursuit of their visions that they will not give up until they have spread their ideas *everywhere*."[6]

Why this development occurred when it did is hard to pin down with certainty, but probable culprits likely include the worldwide spread of education, creating sizable cadres of educated professionals in very unlikely places; the "global associational revolution" that led to a widespread surge of social-change-oriented nongovernmental organizations, or NGOs, able to engage some of these educated professionals;[7] the dot-com explosion with its inspiring message of technological innovation leading to dramatic changes in life-chances; and the networking possibilities created by the new communication technologies and by capacity-building organizations such as Ashoka, which has spent the past several decades identifying and fostering this new breed of actor on the *demand* side of the philanthropic marketplace. Whatever the cause, the result has been to create a mechanism to perform the critical function of translating almost incomprehensible human need into concrete, actionable solutions capable of yielding demonstrable results and attracting the attention of a new breed of socially conscious investors.[8]

Microcredit was the leading edge of this development, and its rapid growth into a $65 billion industry with its own network of microfinance investment funds in the 35 years leading up to 2010 has been a source of inspiration to many of these social entrepreneurs. Indeed, a veritable "fourth sector" has emerged around the world consisting of socially conscious individuals who have discovered novel ways to produce social value out of existing resources in ways that produce real change in the lives of disadvantaged people.[9] They are thus providing inexpensive fresh water, eyeglasses, sanitary pads, housing, healthcare, solar panels, primary education, cell phones, and dozens of other products and services needed by disadvantaged consumers or made by them for sale in other markets.

These social entrepreneurs need capital in order to grow their businesses, and this need is enormous. According to one estimate, of the 365 to 445 million micro, small, or medium-sized firms in developing countries, 70 percent need outside funding but lack access to it.[10] These firms, which generate a third of the GDP and 45 percent of the employment in developing countries, have unmet demands for capital estimated to total $2.1 to $2.5 trillion. This estimate is similar to the estimate cited earlier of $400 billion to $1 trillion in potential demand for capital in businesses serving bottom-of-the-pyramid populations in just five fields (housing, water, maternal health, primary education, and microfinance).[11]

"Social entrepreneurs crystallize need and translate it into concrete projects."

In short, the reality of an enormous number of people living on the edge of economic, environmental, physical, and social disaster, increasingly attracting the attention of innovative social entrepreneurs who are finding new ways to combine existing resources to produce low-cost products and services, but who are confronting constrained resource availability from both government and traditional private philanthropy, translates into a huge demand for the new tools and new actors that we have identified emerging on the new frontiers of philanthropy and social investment.

Supply-Side Factors

But the existence of a large and growing demand for investment capital and other forms of philanthropic innovation is not yet a guarantee that this demand will be met. To the contrary, the current mismatch between needs and resources, even though especially intense in recent years, is hardly a new development. By itself, therefore, it can hardly account for the striking recent emergence of the new actors and tools that we have documented. At best it is a necessary condition for these developments. But it is certainly not a sufficient one. For this latter, supply-side factors are needed as well. What is particularly unique about the present situation is that such factors have not only surfaced, but have mushroomed in the past decade or more. Why is this so?

First Responders and Incentivizers

One important factor, clearly, were the adventurous first responders to the capital needs of early social entrepreneurs, first in the developed Global North, and subsequently in the Global South. These early efforts established a surface plausibility for the idea that it might be possible to find imaginative and workable ideas for solving massive problems of inadequate housing, lagging services, and lack of employment opportunities within the communities experiencing these problems, and to do so in a way that, at a minimum, protected the principal of those providing the upfront capital and, in many cases, offered the prospect of a reasonable rate of financial return. This opened the possibility of attracting not just philanthropic capital, but also actual private investment capital, into such efforts.

Some of the earliest experience in attracting such capital into this type of venture occurred in the housing field in the US. A crucial ingredient here was the series of incentives provided by government policymakers. This included the provisions in the 1969 tax act's payout requirements for charitable foundations authorizing foundations to make program-related investments (PRIs) in for-profit ventures, and to count these toward their required grant-making obligations if they promoted valid foundation objectives. This was followed by a succession of other measures: by the Community Reinvestment Act (CRA) of 1977, which incentivized commercial banks to channel more of their lending into the disadvantaged communities from which they drew significant deposits; by the Low-Income Housing Tax Credit (LIHTC) of 1986, which provided tax credits for private investments in low-income housing; and by the Reigle Community Development and Regulatory Improvement Act of 1994, which fostered the network of Community Development Finance Institutions designed to help channel the funds from banks, insurance companies, and other institutions into valid, community-based housing and community development efforts.

Taken together, these policy steps helped to stimulate a significant flow of private investment capital into low-income housing and community development activity in disadvantaged neighborhoods across the country and to foster a cadre of professionals and institutions with experience tapping private investment resources for social-purpose activities.[12]

Institutions such as the Low Income Support Corporation (LISC) and the Enterprise Foundation emerged to link the providers of finance to the developers of low-income housing and community development projects.

Other early responders included the Calvert Foundation, created in 1988 by a consortium that included Calvert Investments, a socially responsible mutual fund company, and the Ford, MacArthur, and Mott foundations; and the Acumen Fund, established in 2001 with support from the Rockefeller Foundation. Both of these institutions are early examples of what we earlier termed social-impact capital aggregators, generating capital resources from institutional and individual social investors and channeling them to promising social ventures in the US and around the world. The Calvert Foundation currently has nearly $200 million invested in 250 community organizations in all 50 US states and over 100 countries, while Acumen has generated $69 million in investment capital that it has committed to 63 social ventures in eight countries generating an estimated 55,000 jobs.[13]

Along with the network of Community Development Finance Institutions fostered in the US and comparable early community development investment vehicles in other countries, these early responders not only generated important capital to finance developing social enterprises, but also generated something at least equally important: an initial track record of promising innovations and a set of experienced promoters of a new route out of poverty and disadvantage featuring what Acumen Fund describes as "imaginative business solutions" developed by "pioneering entrepreneurs" supported by "investors willing to take on a risk/return profile that is unacceptable to traditional financiers."[14] What is more, they served as prototypes for similar policy innovations in other countries, such as the 2002 Community Investment Tax Relief Scheme in the UK, which fostered a comparable set of community development investment vehicles in that country.

New Concepts: The Fortune at the Bottom of the Pyramid

What gave thrust to the work of these first responders, however, was a second important supply-side development that arose, interestingly enough, in the realm of ideas. Indeed, proving once again the truth of Plato's observation that "ideas rule the world," one of the most significant causes of the revolution in the financing of social-purpose activities in recent years has been the reconceptualization that has occurred about the causes of poverty and how to overcome it. That reconceptualization was spearheaded by the microfinance industry, brought to wide public attention by Nobel laureate Muhammed Yunus, but transformed into a powerful intellectual current by C. K. Prahalad.

"Ideas rule the world."—Plato

Microfinance is, in many respects, an old story, but it is a story that has been repeatedly forgotten since its first appearance in the Irish Loan Fund created by Jonathan Swift in the eighteenth century. As it resurfaced through small-scale lending experiments in Bangladesh and elsewhere in the 1970s, microfinance accomplished a fundamental conceptual breakthrough: it demonstrated that the poor represent a *resource* rather than a liability, and a resource that can generate growth and wealth if approached in the right way. In the case of microfinance, that approach took the form of recognizing in groups of uneducated, poverty-stricken, rural women eager to improve their life circumstances a resource in the form of *peer pressure* that could substitute for absent physical or financial collateral to secure small revolving loan funds through which each of the women in the group could, over time, establish some type of income-earning microenterprise that could propel them down the road toward economic self-sufficiency while enabling them to pay back the loan with interest.

What ultimately lifted this concept of the poor as a resource to takeoff status was a book.

What ultimately lifted this concept to takeoff status was not only the significant international recognition provided through the work of Muhammad Yunus and his Grameen

Bank, or the financial expansion provided by a number of early capital aggregators such as Accion and Kiva, but a book by a University of Michigan corporate-strategy professor of Indian origin by the name of C. K. Prahalad. What Prahalad argued in his 2004 boldly titled book, *The Fortune at the Bottom of the Pyramid*, is that the phenomenon that gave rise to the success of microcredit was not restricted to small-scale lending to groups of rural residents, but rather applied to a wide range of products and services needed by people living in even the direst of poverty, and that such products and services could be delivered to these people at prices far more affordable than they were currently spending while still earning profits for investors and entrepreneurs.[15] This alchemy was possible, Prahalad showed, due to a "penalty" levied on bottom-of-the-pyramid (BOP) consumers as a result of the difficulties and dangers of delivering goods and services to the areas where they live, and the resulting lack of competition to drive prices down. BOP consumers thus end up paying more for the items they consume than do the better-off. Prahalad thus showed that, by designing products and distribution channels that can be accessed by people of limited means who have needs for a variety of products but often pay a premium price, clever entrepreneurs can take advantage of this "bottom-of-the-pyramid penalty" to improve the living conditions and economic prospects for BoP residents while covering their own costs and earning meaningful profits.

New Players/New Mindsets

The crystallization of the idea of a "fortune at the bottom of the pyramid" happened to coincide, moreover, with a third crucial supply-side element: the appearance at the door of the philanthropic arena of a new set of actors that Matthew Bishop and Michael Green have dubbed "philanthrocapitalists"—generally young, dot-com millionaires and billionaires who, having made vast riches relatively early in life, have turned to philanthropy as a way to give back and create value in a different sphere. Bill Gates is doubtless the living icon for this development with his bold decision to retire from his Microsoft day job, establish a large foundation, and turn his energies and intellect to solving the world's problems of poverty and ill-health. Jeffrey Skoll and Pierre Omidyar, founders of e-Bay and early supporters of the social venture phenomenon, are other exemplars of this same phenomenon, as is Charly Kleissner, whose KL Felicitas Foundation is a model of what a foundation that aspires to function as a philanthropic bank looks like.[16]

This group of funders is driven by what Kleisner describes as a "deep responsibility to do something meaningful with the wealth we've created" but also a passion to bring the entrepreneurial style that had stood them in such stead in the world of business to their new social-purpose objectives.[17] Many of them are therefore not content with traditional philanthropy, or at least what they perceive to be traditional philanthropy, and have resolved to transform it, producing a philanthropy that is " 'strategic,' 'market conscious,' 'impact oriented,' 'knowledge-based,' often 'high engagement,' and always driven by the goal of maximizing the 'leverage' of the donor's money."[18] As Bishop and Green put it: "As entrepreneurial 'philanthropreneurs,' they love to back social entrepreneurs who offer innovative solutions to society's problems" and are comfortable with, indeed insistent on, utilizing financing approaches that bring to the world of philanthropy some of the dynamism and leveraging possibilities characteristic of modern corporate finance.

A whole new generation of business school students have been bitten by the social enterprise and social-impact investing bug.

But it is not only dot-com multimillionaires turned philanthrocapitalists who have gotten religion and resolved to turn their attention and their considerable talents and resources to confronting the world's problems. Demographers have identified similar sentiments in two entire new generational clusters—Generation X (those born between 1961 and 81) and the millennials (those born between 1982 and 2001). Unlike their baby boomer parents, these generations are populated disproportionately by people found to be seeking a better balance between work and other aspects of their lives, and to exhibit extraordinary enthusiasm and idealism.[19]

Whatever the truth of these demographic generalizations, there is strong evidence that significant numbers of a whole new generation of business school students and recent graduates have been bitten by the social enterprise and social-impact investing bug, eschewing careers that focus solely on maximizing earnings in place of bringing their business skills to activities with a significant social-purpose dimension. One clear manifestation of this is Net Impact, a 20-year-old organization of young professionals that describes itself as "a community of more than 30,000 change-makers using our jobs to tackle the world's toughest problems, demonstrating that it's possible to make a *net impact* that benefits not just the bottom line—but people and the planet, too."[20] Characteristically enough in our globalized world, Net Impact is a global presence, boasting 300 student and professional chapters worldwide.

Ironically enough, these sentiments seem to have received a significant boost from the 2008 global financial meltdown and ensuing recession. Suddenly, high net worth individuals across a broad front, as well as mom-and-pop investors, had to come to terms with the almost overnight disappearance of substantial portions of their wealth. Whatever the economic impact of this realization, the psychological one seems to have been equally transformative for many. If wealth could disappear so quickly, perhaps accumulating it was not the highest goal one could have in one's life. Perhaps using at least some of it to do good in the world could produce more true value in the form of personal satisfaction, particularly if this could be done in a way that would at least preserve the principal and perhaps even generate a reasonable return.

How fully such sentiments surfaced in the aftermath of the financial crisis is difficult to determine at this point, but the spurt of interest in so-called impact investing among family offices and advisors to high net worth individuals in the wake of the crisis is certainly consistent with the belief that it played a role. What is more, chaos on Wall Street, "the City," and other financial centers also produced more concrete contributions to the growing supply of social capital by releasing thousands of skilled financial experts, some voluntarily and some not so voluntarily, to consider alternative careers. And a number of these skilled professionals were sufficiently burned out by their high-pressure, quick-return, financial-industry experiences to crave opportunities to put their talents and knowledge to work in settings that yielded more personal satisfaction. Not surprisingly, a good number of them found their way into the expanding industry of social-impact capital aggregators.

Emblematic of this development is the career of Pasha Bakhtiar, a Swiss-born researcher who entered the world of traditional investment banking in 1998, earned an MBA, and seemed well on his way to a successful career in this lucrative field, even earning a "Rising Star in Wealth Management" award from *Institutional Investor* in 2007. But in 2010, in the wake of the global financial crisis, Bakhtiar turned his back on the world of traditional investment banking to cofound Willow Impact Investors, a social-impact investment firm that aggregates capital for investments in what it terms for-profit companies "committed to generating positive, sustainable, and demonstrable social and environmental impact while complying with a commercial imperative."[21]

The financial crisis…made social-impact investments look good.

Financial Crisis: Limited Alternative Investments

The financial crisis and ensuing recession contributed to the supply side of the social capital market in an even more direct way as well: it made social-impact investments look good by transforming them into some of the most profitable investments available. It did so, of course, not by boosting the returns on social-impact investments but by deflating the returns on other types of investments. With global stock markets staggering, the financial industry experiencing rapid disintermediation, and interest rates on everything from US treasuries to certificates of deposit plummeting to historic lows, social-impact investments that offered even 3–4 percent returns and default rates that looked like the gold standard next to previously prized junk bonds and derivatives emerged as some of the most attractive investment options available. And many of these problems persisted for more than four years. The year 2013 thus opened with money managers and investors complaining of suffering from "battered investor syndrome" as they looked out at money market accounts yielding barely a half of a percentage point of interest, two-year certificates of deposit under 1 percent, 10-year US treasuries under 2 percent, and global stock markets barely back to where they had been five years earlier.[22] Doubtless some of the $4.4 billion in social-impact investments clocked in 2011, not to mention the $2.5 billion invested in 2010, was motivated at least in part by invidious comparisons with the returns available from more traditional investments, especially with respected investment firms such as J.P. Morgan reporting both expected and realized returns on social-impact investments in line with relevant market benchmarks.[23]

Infrastructure

Building on the contributions of these first responders and new converts has been a concerted effort to create an infrastructure to support the new frontiers of philanthropy. To be sure, as noted earlier, a robust set of infrastructure organizations had already surfaced in this arena by the turn of the twentieth century into the twenty-first. The Opportunity Finance Network, the Social Investment Forum (SIF), the Consultative Group to Assist the Poor (CGAP), the PRI Makers Network, More for Mission, the Microfinance Investment Exchange, and the International Association of Microfinance Investors (IAMFI) are just a few of the entities created in the past decade or two to promote the new actors and new tools surfacing in the social investing arena.

Notwithstanding this profusion of infrastructure organizations, however, a group of foundations, development agencies, and private financial institutions convened by the Rockefeller Foundation in a series of key gatherings in 2007 and 2008 came to the conclusion that a broader field-building effort was still needed that could bring these various separate initiatives together under a common umbrella and move the field beyond what one pair of authors termed "uncoordinated innovation."[24] The upshot was the launch in 2009 of yet another infrastructure organization called GIIN, the Global Impact Investing Network, but this time with substantial funding from the Rockefeller Foundation, J.P. Morgan, and the US Agency for International Development.

The GIIN was charged with the task of accelerating the development of the social-impact investing industry by creating critical infrastructure, improving practice, establishing a common language, and stimulating field-building research. As noted earlier, to do so, it has established an "Investors' Council" made up of leading impact investors from around the world; created so-called Impact Reporting and Investment Standards (IRIS), a broad set of indicators through which social-impact investors can measure the social performance of their investments; established an online database of impact investment funds called "ImpactBase" to facilitate collaboration among funds working in similar fields and geographies; and carried out a variety of outreach efforts to elevate the visibility of the field and encourage its expansion, including research designed to establish social-impact investing as an "asset class" with its own skill requirements, organizational structures, metrics, trade groups, and educational offerings.[25]

Technology has effectively made it possible to bring the supply of capital virtually to the doorstep of the social entrepreneurs in need of it.

Technology

Finally, the appearance and growth of the new frontiers of philanthropy chronicled here has been significantly enhanced by the vast advances in communication technology over the past two decades. This technology has effectively made it possible to bring the supply of capital virtually to the doorstep of the social entrepreneurs in need of it, and for organizations such as the Calvert Foundation and Acumen Fund to assemble significant portfolios of investment capital from contributions with denominations as small as $20. In addition, the new technology has significantly reduced one of the major causes of the so-called bottom-of-the-pyramid penalty, access to BOP consumers. In the process, it has rendered a variety of BOP business models far more viable than they could otherwise ever have been. As Churchill and Peterson show in Chapter 17 in the companion volume to this book, for example, technology is enabling providers of microinsurance to reach the BOP market on a mass basis thanks to the availability of mobile phones, smart cards, and new payment systems. Online giving and investment portals such as Kiva and Network for Good would similarly not have been possible were it not for the technological advances.

Summary

In short, there is reason to believe that the recent changes taking place on the frontiers of philanthropy are more than a passing fad. Some significant underlying forces have been at work to produce this development at this time. What is more, these forces are operating both on the demand side of this evolving market—creating a strong need for the changes that are underway—and on the supply side—stimulating the availability of both the talents and the finances to meet this need.

Some of these forces are admittedly ephemeral (one can hope, for example, that global markets will return at some point to a greater degree of normalcy). But others appear more durable—the new excitement about the BOP market, foundations' interest in expanding the leverage they can get out of their resources, the new attitudes and new actors taking an active role in social and environmental problem-solving, and the maturation of social-impact investments as an asset class.

But none of this means that the road ahead for these developments is clear of obstacles. To the contrary, significant challenges remain. It is to these that we must therefore now turn.

Chapter 5

Remaining Obstacles

The discussion to this point has painted an enormously positive picture of the potential consequences of the changes taking place on the frontiers of philanthropy and social investing. More than that, it has documented some underlying factors that appear to be driving these changes and giving them durability, thus enhancing the possibility that they can achieve the enormous breakthroughs they promise in the lives of millions of disadvantaged people throughout the world.

Considerable obstacles still confront the developments on the new frontiers of philanthropy.

But no clear-eyed assessment of these developments can proceed very far without acknowledging the considerable obstacles that these developments also still confront. These obstacles take a number of forms, but five of them seem especially important to acknowledge and, ultimately, confront.

No Good Deed Goes Unpunished: Normative Implications of the New Frontiers

In the first place, it is important to recognize that the shift in the locus of decision-making responsibility for allocating social-purpose resources from charitable foundations and government program officers to private-sector investment managers, and the new investment focus and metrics-oriented emphasis that this will bring with it, does not come without distributional consequences. Simply put, there will be winners and losers resulting from this shift in the locus of responsibility, and in the criteria for allocating resources, in the social-purpose arena. And not all of these consequences will best serve the social-purpose objectives claimed for the new-frontier initiatives.

As Mike Edwards reminds us in Part A of Chapter 20 of our companion volume, performance metrics give inherent advantages to some types of interventions over others, and these are not always the interventions with the greatest social impact. Impact measures, for example, tend to be short term in nature, rarely extending beyond a year or two. Significant social change, however, often takes five or 10 years. Do we really want to tie ourselves to assessment regimes that systematically disadvantage initiatives with the greatest chance of achieving long-run change?

Some of the most profound improvements in the lives of disadvantaged people result not from the provision of particular services but from the elimination of unequal structures of power and barriers to opportunity.

In addition, the investment orientation and metrics emphasis of the new frontiers give an advantage to service activities—providing healthcare, or food, or electricity to people. But past experience has shown that some of the most profound improvements in the lives of disadvantaged people result not from the provision of particular services but from the elimination of unequal structures of power and barriers to opportunity, and these require vigorous advocacy efforts instead. This is the lesson, for example, of the American civil rights movement. Civil rights organizations were not in the business of providing housing, or needed healthcare, or education to the country's African-American citizens. They could therefore hardly have had much appeal to social-impact investors fixated on these tangible manifestations of social impacts as the major criteria for success. But the truth is that their ultimate impact on the life-chances of millions upon millions of America's African-American citizens easily trumped that of any number of narrow service initiatives with strong two- or even four-year performance records. Fortunately, however, there were enlightened foundations and individual people of conscience willing to support the advocacy campaigns that opened the doors of opportunity through which tens of thousands of America's African-American citizens have been able to walk since then. Will all the hype and enthusiasm generated by the "new frontiers" phenomenon draw too much attention and resources away from the similar advocacy efforts still required to break down oppressive structures of power and barriers to opportunity? Without confronting these dilemmas, the social-impact investment movement can easily find itself running afoul of the very social change impulses it is claiming to be advancing.

The Conundrum of Social-Impact Measurement

One way to protect against the risks of mission creep inevitably involved in pursuing social-purpose objectives through market means is to build in performance standards for the social-purpose objectives that are every bit as stringent as those for the financial objectives of such investments. To their credit, the promoters of the new social-impact investment movement recognized the need for such social-purpose performance standards and have launched a variety of efforts to develop them. To date, however, these efforts remain what Brian Trelstad, a prominent leader in this field, describes as still "an elusive quest."[1] Despite the compelling logic of the concept of "blended value," or blended return, embracing financial, social, and environmental elements, this concept remains merely a powerful metaphor since no tool yet exists to measure reliably the blended return on philanthropic investments, and certainly none that can compare the relative blended returns across a diverse set of interventions.

The formulation of a reliable way to measure social impact remains, at best, a "work in progress."

Much of the work to date has focused on formulating a common taxonomy of potential social, environmental, and financial performance indicators. The most ambitious of these taxonomies is the Impact Reporting and Investment Standards (IRIS), supported by the Rockefeller Foundation and developed under the auspices of the Global Impact Investing Network. This taxonomy includes more than 400 indicators in terms of which social-impact investors can demonstrate the social and environmental, as well as financial, performance of their investments. As noted earlier, however, the dilemma is that with so many different indicators against which social performance can be demonstrated, the performance measurement system comes to resemble those grade-school drawing contests designed so that the number of prizes is large enough to send every child home a winner.

To get around this problem, the creators of IRIS have joined forces with B-Lab, a nonprofit organization involved in identifying and promoting so-called benefit corporations, to create a rating system for social-impact investments and investors.[2] Called the Global Impact Investing Rating System, or GIIRS, this system rates companies in terms of their performance in four major areas—corporate governance, treatment of workers, impact on the environment, and role in the community, including patterns of supply-chain management and diversity of the workforce—giving companies a composite score based on answers to 50–120 weighted questions.[3] The system thus bears marked resemblance to the various corporate social responsibility reporting systems that are part of the socially responsible investing and purchasing movement.[4]

While these developments are promising, most observers are in agreement with Trelstad in seeing the formulation of a reliable way to measure social impact to be what one author calls, at best, a "work in progress."[5] What is more, the take-up of nonfinancial performance measures remains limited among investors. Thornley and Dailey, writing in 2010, reported "limited evidence" of reporting on nonfinancial performance by most investors in their annual reports, with anecdotal reporting the most prevalent form of reporting by those who do report.[6] O'Donohue et al. found a similar dearth of serious nonfinancial performance reporting among a surveyed group of "impact investors," with only 2 percent using a third-party impact measurement system, and the rest using, at best, their own proprietary systems or the systems used by their investees.[7]

This is understandable enough given how complicated, expensive, and subjective nonfinancial performance measurement can be, but it could lead the field in the wrong direction. Many close observers of social-purpose activity endorse an approach to measuring the impact of this work that I have elsewhere termed "What would Google do?" And what Google would do is to focus on the user, to assess impact by asking the people who are meant to benefit from an investment.[8] Instead, prominent experts in the social-impact investing world have proposed what they term an "investor-centered" approach to building social-impact performance measurement systems. But this leaves the field of social-impact investing vulnerable to false claims of social impact and the potential for significant mission creep as standard financial performance measures come to trump more uncertain and costly nonfinancial ones. Indeed, there is already evidence of such pressures in the social enterprise field. Thus, a recent survey of 25 social ventures in the US found that 22 experienced "significant conflicts" between their missions and the demands of corporate stakeholders, and that the two that were most successful financially reported deviating most significantly from their social mission by reducing the time devoted to advocacy, weeding out the most needy, and hence most costly, clients, and focusing on activities with the greatest revenue-generating potential.[9]

Still a Boutique Business

Quite apart from the challenge it faces in demonstrating its social-impact bona fides to skeptics, the social-impact investment movement has also not quite succeeded in making the "sale" to its primary audience: mainline institutional investors such as pension funds, insurance companies, sovereign wealth funds, and major corporations.[10] To be sure, important progress has been made, with an estimated $8.0 billion in new impact investments clocked in 2012 according to recent data assembled by J.P. Morgan Social Finance and GIIN, up from $4.4 billion in 2011, and $2.5 billion in 2010, with a projected increase to $9.1 billion in 2014.[11] What is more, new funding intermediaries are forming on an increasingly global scale, as the earlier discussion indicated.

The social-impact investment movement has not quite succeeded in making the sale to its primary audience: mainline institutional investors.

Impressive as this progress is, however, it is well to remember that $8 billion is still well under one-twentieth of 1 percent of the $14,442 billion of assets just in US commercial banks, less than one-tenth of 1 percent of the $7,963 billion of assets in US mutual funds, and just slightly over one-tenth of 1 percent of the $6,080 billion of assets in US pension funds.[12] And that is just US capital markets. A World Economic Forum report issued in September 2013 confirms this basic point and identifies this limited penetration of social-impact investing into the world's mainstream capital markets as threatening to tag the social-impact investing movement as little more than " 'a hype,' " or passing fad.[13]

As Mary Tingerthal reports in Chapter 14 of our companion volume, advocates of low-income housing and community development finance, who have dreamed of tapping the highly promising tool of asset-backed securities to finance the revitalization of ailing communities, have so far found this dream "largely unrealized."[14] Even in the field of international microfinance, which has attracted considerable private-sector funding, the ability to leverage resources by "securitizing" debt instruments remains in its infancy: only 12 percent of the $4.2 billion in debt instruments held by microfinance investment intermediaries internationally, and less than 1 percent of total microcredit loans outstanding, have been assembled into debt instruments that can be sold to investors in order to refresh the makers of microfinance loans.

The subfield of "sustainable and responsible investing," which covers entities that apply some type of environmental, social, or governance criteria to their investments, has attained greater scale. The most recent data found $3.7 trillion of assets managed against such screens in the US.[15] This is a much less active form of utilizing assets for social and environmental purposes, however. Even so, it still represents a fairly modest 2.6 percent of all financial assets in US financial institutions.

The reasons for this slow climb are not hard to discern and have been recognized from the outset. Among the factors well rehearsed in the literature are the relative immaturity of many social enterprises, the limited experience of many of the management teams, the novelty of some of the investment vehicles, and the enormous uncertainties surrounding the liquidity of the investments due to the lack of tested exit opportunities. Add to this the inevitable country risk factors, the exchange rate risk factors, the high transaction costs, and the lack of clear data on investment returns and it is easy to see why social finance remains today what Federal Reserve Bank official David Erickson calls a "boutique business," and why three-fourths of the respondents to a recent J.P. Morgan survey of impact investors concluded that this industry, while "growing," is nevertheless "still in its infancy."[16]

The Pesky Issue of Deal Flow

Another factor inhibiting the growth of the social-impact investment market arises not from the supply side of the market in the form of investor reticence, but from the demand side in the form of investee absence. How can this be so? After all, as noted previously, of the estimated 365 to 445 million micro, small, and medium-sized firms in developing countries, 70 percent need, but do not have, access to external funding, and this does not even include the informal enterprises so numerous in these countries. Why are these enterprises not pressing their claims for capital on the increasingly plentiful sources of it?

Inefficiencies in the social capital market, skill deficits on the part of investees, and the sheer difficulty of BOP businesses conspire to limit investment demand.

Broadly speaking, three main lines of explanation of this apparent paradox can be identified. The first such line of explanation focuses on inefficiencies in the social capital markets. Such markets have long been fragmented, disjointed, relatively small, and therefore difficult to access. Even with the new technologies, the geographical, physical, conceptual, and psychological distances between the 400 million small entrepreneurs in need of capital and the relative handful of social capital aggregators in a position to deploy it remains measured in light-years. Add to that the significant costs of due diligence and structuring transactions and it is easy to see why the flow of investible deals remains somewhat anemic despite the clear need.

The second line of explanation for why impact investors continue to identify a "shortage of quality investment opportunities" as one of the top two most serious challenges they face relates less to the inefficiencies of the market than to the skill deficits on the part of potential investees.[17] The entities involved in social-purpose activities are typically nonprofit organizations, small-scale mom-and-pop enterprises, faith-based charities, cooperatives, mutual societies, and courageous, individual social entrepreneurs. Few are schooled in the basics of finance. As outlined in a recent Venturesome report, many lack a clear understanding of the difference between operating income and investment capital, are unable to identify their own financial needs with precision, are unschooled in the different financial instruments available to them, and are unaware of how to assemble multiple sources of finance into manageable funding packages.[18] This lack of basic financial literacy leaves a yawning gulf between the seekers of capital, who tend to bring forward, at best, micro deals, and the potential providers of it, who are accustomed to operating at a scale orders of magnitude larger than this. And it is a gulf that those involved in building the social-impact investing industry have curiously neglected to address very coherently in their zeal to bring the new investors to the table first.[19]

It is perhaps the third line of explanation for the lagging deal flow in the impact investing market that is the most damning, however. Simply put, there are too few deals because the BOP market, for all its promise, is an enormously difficult market in which to operate, and certainly in which to operate at a profit while adhering to meaningful social-purpose objectives. Harvey Koh and colleagues identify the situation well when they describe the "heavy burden" that firms pioneering new business models in BOP environments regularly confront:

> *They must develop and refine their models the hard way, by trying them out in an unforgiving, low-margin marketplace. Inevitably they suffer failures and setbacks on the road to viability. Often they also have to invest heavily in educating customers about the possibilities of new "push" solutions and in developing unskilled suppliers and fragmented distribution channels to serve their requirements. Although excited by their novelty, investors are often rattled by the firms' risk profiles and are unimpressed by their financial returns, all the while suspecting that they might actually be savvy nonprofits masquerading as commercially viable models.[20]*

A "pioneer gap" confronts the social-purpose market, limiting the supply of investible deals able to absorb the pent-up supply of social investment capital.

Despite the optimistic assumptions about the enormous flow of resources poised to pour into promising bottom-of-the-pyramid businesses, the task of bringing such businesses to the point of attracting serious capital is a long and tortuous one. As Koh and his colleagues point out, it took the Grameen Bank 17 years to break even after its launch in 1976, and other trajectories have proven equally demanding. The Acumen Fund has had to filter through more than 5,000 companies over 10 years to find 65 promising enough to invest in, and this with a set of financial return expectations that is highly conservative by investment standards. Indeed, the average after-tax profit of Acumen's portfolio companies remains underwater. And no wonder. Monitor Group research in India suggests that it takes 10 years for an inclusive social enterprise to achieve a scale sufficient to generate profitable operations.[21]

Given this situation, social-impact investors have shied away from the early financing of promising BOP businesses. But this creates a classic "free rider" problem: while all investors would benefit from joint support of promising businesses during their early, uncertain start-up phases, no particular investor can see it in its interest to do so for any particular promising business since once its concept is proved, multiple competitors will swoop into the market to benefit from the initial investment without sharing in the cost. The result is what Koh and colleagues term "the pioneer gap," the absence of funding to support the critical start-up phase of promising social ventures and the resulting lack of sufficient investible deals to absorb the pent-up supply of social investment capital.

Just as in other cases of such "market failures," what is needed in such circumstances is a nonmarket solution to the market imperfection. Traditionally, this role is played by government in cases of other so-called collective goods, such as national defense, and government can play a critical role here as well. The UK's Department for International Development, for example, provided crucial early-stage financing for the M-PESA mobile phone electronic payment system that has brought financial services for the first time to 9 million Kenyan residents. The US Agency for International Development provided similar assistance in the early development of clean-burning cooking stoves in Ghana.[22]

But given the political risks of choosing successful technologies or business models, responsibility for overcoming this particular market imperfection may more properly belong to the institutions we earlier referred to as "foundations as philanthropic banks," that is, foundations willing to tap their endowments as well as their grant budgets to leverage their resources for maximum impact on the causes they have chosen to advance. Koh and his colleagues refer to this as "enterprise philanthropy," but we might just as well refer to it colloquially as "PRIs on steroids." It essentially involves identifying highly promising BOP business propositions that have gotten beyond the initial proof of concept and helping them to validate the commercial viability of their products, prepare the market for their launch, and get them into initial operation in order to facilitate the eventual investment of private, return-seeking capital that can bring the resulting businesses to scale.[23] Such support can take the form of grants, but it might equally take the form of low-interest or no-interest loans, or noncontrolling equity.

Getting Beyond Comforting Assumptions

What the discussion above suggests is that those promoting, or operating on, the new frontiers of philanthropy may be approaching a moment of truth. Many of the developments identified here have been launched with enormous fanfare and enormous hope. Long-standing tensions between doing good and doing well were miraculously being suspended; market rates of return were available from activities pursued with the intention of achieving social and environmental progress; private investment markets were available to replace government and private charities as the principal sources of social-purpose growth capital; and a new era of social-purpose finance was just around the corner.

Three comforting assumptions [of] social-impact investing...have now been significantly challenged.

These assertions have hardly been disproved. Indeed, the developments outlined in this monograph, and in its companion volume, retain considerable momentum and immense promise. Still, the field has achieved sufficient maturity to be able to acknowledge the hard slog that still lies ahead. In particular, three comforting assumptions that have helped to fuel the hype around social-impact investing, as well as some of the other innovations on the frontiers of philanthropy, have now been significantly challenged, if not completely refuted, and the resulting realities must now be confronted as the field moves into the next phase of its development.

Traditional Market Risk-Return Ratios?

In the first place, many of the return expectations broadcast in the early literature on social-impact investing seem overly optimistic and unsupported by the actual experience of the pioneers operating in the field. To be sure, there are powerful examples of BOP businesses that are producing significant social benefit while generating impressive market returns. But those businesses required years of painful incubation before they sprang into view as mature enterprises achieving the returns for which they are now celebrated in the literature. Yet this long and costly incubation is too often discounted or totally ignored, as are the dozens of other promising business offspring that never survived the embryo stage. While it may not be the case, as Kevin Starr has warned, that "there's really only one bottom line—it's either impact or profit, and the demands of investors can pull an organization away from the target population toward those able to pay more," the fact remains that enticing investors with the returns achieved by the handful of success stories can create expectations that can easily move the field in this direction.[24]

The solution here need not be to give up on the promise of social-impact investing and the mobilization of private investment capital for social and environmental purposes. Rather, the solution is to recognize the need for more complex financial packages in order to accommodate the financial return needs of private investors without ignoring the exceptional risk profiles facing most start-up businesses serving BOP markets.

A Substitute for Government?

This brings us to a second comforting assumption that has crept into the new frontiers of philanthropy mindset. This is the assumption that social-impact investing, the mobilization of private investment capital for social and environmental purposes, can significantly substitute for lagging governmental resources and involvement. To be sure, the ideology of privatism has a long lineage in American political thought, and particularly so in the philanthropic arena.[25] It should come as no surprise, therefore, that a potent theme in the "philanthrocapitalism" playbook is the suggestion that just as the private sector can "do it better than government" in running businesses and generating profits, so too it can do the same in advancing social and environmental objectives. Government is therefore not needed, or at least not needed as much, in this arena.

Unlocking capital for social-purpose activity turns out to require a crowbar.

This assumption, too, however, finds little support in the evidence. If it takes a village to rear a child, it appears to take a virtual cabinet of government departments to generate even a small trickle of private investment capital into social-purpose activities. This, at any rate, is the experience in the one field of social purpose investment in the US that has attracted perhaps the most substantial, if still small, flow of such capital— that is, affordable housing and community development. To stimulate and sustain that flow of funds has required the joint actions of no fewer than seven government agencies: the US Congress, the Board of Governors of the Federal Reserve System (FRB), the Federal Deposit Insurance Corporation (FDIC), the Office of the Comptroller of the Currency (OCC), the Office of Thrift Supervision (OTS), the Internal Revenue Service, and the Community Development Financial Institutions Fund in the Department of the Treasury. These officials have responsibility for administering four different programs that have been needed to get private investment capital flowing into inner cities and affordable housing. As described earlier, these are the Community Reinvestment Act (CRA), incentivizing bank investments in distressed communities; the Low-Income Housing Tax Credit, which offers tax credits to investors in low-income housing; the Community Development Financial Institutions Fund, which supports the nationwide network of CDFIs; and the New Markets Tax Credit, which provides tax breaks to investors in distressed areas.

As we have seen, public-sector funding, or other forms of assistance, provided either directly or through multinational development banks, has been equally important in helping to nudge private-sector investors into participation in social-purpose efforts in other settings as well, including the UK and in much of the developing world. Unlocking capital for social-purpose activity turns out to require a crowbar and often the kind of muscle and resources that governments alone can wield. While no one can doubt the crucial role that private capital can, and is, playing, no one either can realistically expect the private sector to do it on its own.

Goodbye to Traditional Philanthropy?

Finally, from what has been said, it should be clear that the predictions of the imminent demise of traditional philanthropy that have accompanied the rise of social-impact investment in some quarters are as exaggerated as the ones that reached Mark Twain announcing his untimely death. As the discussion of the "pioneer gap" and the need for complex financing "tranches" make clear, the new world of social-impact investing requires the old world of traditional philanthropy in order to succeed. The one cannot easily function without the other.

This is not to say that traditional philanthropy can be maximally helpful if it continues to function in traditional ways. Rather, traditional philanthropy will have to change if it wishes to remain fully relevant in the new world of social-purpose finance that is emerging. It will need to function as a catalyst for more complicated funding consortia. It will need to partner with other types of funding institutions, both public and private. And it will need to learn how to combine its traditional tool of grants with other resources of its own, and with the resources of other types of institutions, to achieve the leverage needed to gain traction on the serious problems the world confronts. In philanthropy as well as in other spheres, the world of "either-or" must be replaced by the practice of "both-and."

Chapter 6

Prescription: The Way Forward

From what has been reported here it should be clear that the new frontiers of philanthropy hold enormous promise for gaining meaningful traction on a wide range of social, economic, and environmental problems facing the world at the present time. To be sure, the solutions on offer from many of the new developments taking place on the frontiers of philanthropy and social investing may not be appropriate for all problems or all locations. One recent analysis suggested, for example, four key conditions that must be met for social-impact investment to work properly: (1) the issue or problem should be of a scale that makes it unlikely that either government or philanthropy will have the resources alone to address it; (2) there must be a viable market-based solution available or in reasonable prospect; (3) mainstream private investors should not already be heavily engaged; and (4) market-based solutions must be considered morally acceptable.[1] Clearly, not all of the globe's challenges, and perhaps not even the most severe of them, will meet these criteria. What is more, even those that do will stumble along the way because many of the new techniques have their own problems: their complexity deters many potential participants, standards for ensuring valid social outcomes are not fully developed, and investors with the patience to wait out the lengthy proof-of-concept phase of social-purpose investments may not be forthcoming.

"Despite obstacles and limitations, there is sufficient promise...to warrant further active encouragement."

Yet, despite these limitations, observers have identified a number of areas where these new actors and tools enjoy significant potential, and new such areas are being discovered on a regular basis. Included are such areas as housing, health-care, education, utilities, agriculture, financial services, and insurance. In all of these, imaginative products such as low-cost solar panels, modular housing, cheap eyeglasses, reusable sanitary napkins, and clean-burning stoves are transforming lives while generating at least modest profits for investors and entrepreneurs. In short, despite the obstacles and limitations, there is sufficient promise in the developments taking place on the frontiers of philanthropy to warrant further active encouragement of them.

But what form should such encouragement take? Based on the discussion here, six steps seem especially worth pursuing.

Visualize

In the first place, there remains a significant need to enable more people to visualize and grasp the dramatic changes underway on what we have termed the "new frontiers of philanthropy." The developments portrayed in this book are diffuse and diverse. It is therefore all too easy for people to miss the forest for the trees, indeed to fail to comprehend that there is a substantial forest at all. Drawing a circle around these developments and finding a way to portray them coherently is thus the first step toward allowing the various stakeholders involved—individual investors, investment managers, financial institutions, social entrepreneurs, philanthropic institutions, nonprofit managers, and the general public—to appreciate the enormity of the changes and to begin to position themselves more actively in relation to them. Hopefully, this monograph and its companion volume, with their systematic identification and analysis of a sizable range of the new actors and tools that are emerging, will contribute usefully to this visualization goal and to the action that will hopefully flow from it.

Publicize

Visualization is just a first step toward the broader awareness-raising needed to bring the message of the new frontiers to the various groups of stakeholders whose involvement holds the key to its promise. For this, a much more robust educational and field-broadening effort will be required.

To be sure, some components of the new frontiers phenomenon have begun to achieve meaningful scale in terms of the numbers of institutions engaged. The Forum for Sustainable and Responsible Investing (US SIF Foundation) thus identifies 443 institutional investors, 272 money managers, and over

1,000 community investment institutions such as community development financial institutions and credit unions in the US alone that are applying various environmental, social, and corporate governance (ESG) criteria to their investment analysis and portfolio selection as of the end of 2011, and 200 of these institutions filed or cofiled shareholder resolutions on these issues at publicly traded companies from 2010 through 2012.[2]

Despite a substantial investment of time and resources, this field remains...well off the beaten path of mainline philanthropy and much of private investment, and virtually unknown to all but the most intrepid nonprofit explorers.

But though impressive, these numbers are hardly overwhelming, especially given that the sustainable and responsible investing movement had its start four decades ago and is a less demanding form of activity than the more direct forms of social-impact investing identified in this volume. Especially striking is the limited involvement on the part of foundations, which are institutions with clear social objectives that could be advanced by the use of social, environmental, and good-corporate governance screens on their investment portfolios. Yet US SIF was able to identify only 95 out of the country's 76,545 foundations—a mere one-tenth of 1 percent of the foundations—that reported applying ESG criteria to their investments. And only $60.3 billion of the total $590.2 billion in foundation assets—or about 10 percent of the total— is definitively subject to such criteria as a consequence.[3]

Elsewhere, knowledge of the developments outlined here remains hit-or-miss at best, even among critical stakeholders, such as foundations, investment managers, pension funds, mutual fund firms, and nonprofit organizations across a broad array of fields. The social-impact investing component of this new development is particularly in need of broader communication and awareness-raising. As evidence of this, a 2013 survey by CFA Institute, the largest association of investment professionals in the world, found that two-thirds of financial advisers surveyed confessed to being unaware of "impact investing."[4] In short, despite a substantial investment of time and resources, this field remains a distant subcontinent, well off the beaten path of mainline philanthropy and much of private investment, and virtually unknown to all but the most intrepid nonprofit explorers.

To overcome this, it will be necessary to take information on the new frontiers of philanthropy out to a broader strata of participants and observers, to bring knowledge of the new tools and actors "from the margins to the mainstream," as a recent World Economic Forum document recently put it.[5] This will require new materials that can penetrate the academic settings where the next generations of nonprofit executives, money managers, and foundation officials are being trained, as well as new "mainstream messengers" capable of serving, as two prominent advocates of the field have recognized, as "the conduits that can absorb the lessons from visionary practice and communicate them effectively to much wider audiences,"[6] a task that this book, and the field-broadening efforts that can flow from it, has set for itself, and that others will hopefully help it achieve.

Incentivize

A third important encouragement needed is outright incentivization. A key conclusion of recent work assessing the early history of some of the emerging new forms of philanthropy and social investment is the continued importance of credit enhancements, regulatory requirements, tax breaks, and other forms of incentives for these new tools to live up to their promise of delivering meaningful social, economic, and environmental gains to disadvantaged populations and regions while still attracting the involvement of private investors. The long gestation period of microcredit, the "pioneer gap" facing most other BOP products before they become commercially viable, and the array of regulatory requirements, tax advantages, and grants that was required to stimulate a flow of private investment capital into affordable housing in the US all speak volumes about the need to engage other actors beyond the private investors who have been the featured actors in the hype recently surrounding social-impact investment.

In a sense, the rhetoric of social-impact investing has come full circle over just the past half-decade. Initially promoting the new, market-based, social investment instruments as a way to fill in for lagging government and traditional philanthropic support of social and environmental problem-solving, advocates of these new, market-based instruments have recently come to the realization that government and institutional philanthropy are actually not only important, but "doubly important," to the success of the market-based approaches.[7] Increasingly needed are complex funding "stacks" that combine grants, unsecured loans, and various forms of guarantees, subsidies, and occasionally regulations provided by governments and charitable foundations in order to unleash the flow of private investment capital and to make complex undertakings possible.

The rhetoric of social-impact investing has come full circle regarding the relative roles of the private market, government, and foundations.

For this to be possible, however, both governments and foundations will need to alter their current modus operandi. Governments in the US and the UK have begun to do this, albeit only in selective spheres. Elsewhere, the environment for the new approaches outlined here is often more restrictive. Credit enhancements from external sources that lower the interest rate on loans to social entrepreneurs in India, for example, are disallowed by laws prohibiting external loans at rates below those offered by the Bank of India. Elsewhere, foundation support of for-profit businesses is prohibited or discouraged even if the businesses advance the social-purpose missions of the foundations, while laws permitting companies to seek a balance between social purpose and financial return are nonexistent in many places. Coherent efforts to eliminate legal and other impediments and institute positive incentives for the kinds of investment in social-purpose activities described here will thus be necessary, as Shirley Sagawa argues convincingly in Chapter 24 of our companion volume.[8]

So, too, will be a willingness on the part of more foundations to join the ranks of foundations as "philanthropic banks" outlined above and described more completely in Chapter 5 of our companion volume. They, too, will be needed to join the public-private investment consortia that the new actors and tools make possible, to tap into their full asset base, and to make use of a wider array of tools of action than traditional one-off grants.

Legitimize

For these incentives to be forthcoming, however, more progress will be needed in developing the social-impact performance standards that can fully legitimize government and foundation support for the new forms of social investment. Because they are utilizing market means and potentially generating market-rate returns to at least some of their investors, social-impact investing, as well as some of the other new forms of philanthropy and social-purpose activity, must be even more vigilant than traditional philanthropy about retaining public trust. Demonstrating their social-purpose bona fides will therefore be a perennial, and growing, challenge for such initiatives, particularly if the hoped-for return rates begin to materialize, a point that early supporters of these initiatives have clearly recognized.[9]

If the field is serious about its nonfinancial performance indicators, it will need to broaden its approach.

To date, however, the field has yet to produce what the pivotal 2009 Monitor report identified as a "standard-setting body that would help create a threshold for what would be considered an impact investment."[10] Although a standard-setting body has been established, its criteria tend to mirror broader corporate social responsibility criteria rather than targeted thresholds for what can be considered an impact investment. And while targeted impact measures have been identified, they are not attached to a standard-setting body establishing thresholds and are at any rate so numerous that almost any investment seems likely to be able to justify itself as a social impact one in terms of them.

If the field is serious about its nonfinancial performance indicators, it will need to broaden its approach. Instead of focusing its search on "investor-centered" indicators, as some have suggested, it will need to focus at least equal attention on indicators that are convincing to the two chief sources of the incentives these tools have proven to need in order to function effectively: government and private philanthropy. And this will likely involve some way to bring the constituencies of these investments more actively into the performance measurement picture, something that none of the extant performance systems does.

A fairly robust training effort is required to attend to the critical issue of deal flow.

Capacitize

A fifth step needed to capture the promise resident in the new frontiers of philanthropy is to attend to the critical issue of deal flow. This will require more than visualizing and publicizing the new opportunities. Also required is serious training to build what one observer has called the "investment readiness" of actual or potential entrepreneurs.[11] Many of the personnel in position to access the new resources potentially available through the new frontiers of philanthropy are lacking the rudimentary financial knowledge to do so effectively. They are often managers of nonprofit organizations, community organizers, or microbusiness owners. Most of their experience is in the world of grant funding or small-scale bank lending. A fairly robust training effort is therefore required to prepare such organizations and personnel to generate deals that meet the market tests required for the new tools of social investment.

A report by the UK social investment fund Venturesome, for example, identified a broad range of issues facing social investees in the UK as they seek to negotiate the new financial environment in which they find themselves. As reflected in Box 6.1, these include some basic financial skills and basic financial awareness. Left unattended, they will continue to impede the realization of the promise that social-impact investing holds out.

Hopefully, this book and its companion volume will provide material that can begin to remedy these shortcomings, but some energetic outreach will be needed to put the materials to work.

> ## Box 6.1
> ## Key Gaps in Knowledge on the Part of Potential Social Investees
>
> (i)   an inability to identify their own financial needs;
> (ii)   lack of understanding of the difference between operating income and capital;
> (iii) lack of awareness of the financial instruments available and the relative pros and cons of each;
> (iv) limited awareness of the different capital providers available to them;
> (v)   failure to recognize that grants are not free money, but rather involve significant costs; and
> (vi) lack of confidence and knowledge to structure deals blending different investor appetites and instruments.
>
> *Source*: Emilie Goodall and John Kingston, *Access to Capital: A Briefing Paper* (London: CAF Venturesome, 2009), 4, accessed February 10, 2013, http://www.marmanie.com/cms/upload/file/CAF_Venturesome_Access_to_Capital_0909.pdf.

Actualize

Finally, at the end of the day, what is needed is the hard task of doing deals, of scouting the terrain of promising social innovations, deciding which ones might hold promise of becoming commercially viable while generating significant social or environmental payoff, supporting them through the treacherous proof-of-concept phase, assessing their realistic capital and managerial needs, amassing the needed combination of financial and technical assistance, and taking the resulting concepts to scale. Clearly, the transaction costs of this set of tasks are enormous. It is no wonder, then, that a recent status report on the social-impact investing "industry" identified "placing and managing capital" as one of the six top challenges the field faces.[12]

This challenge will not likely be met by social-impact investors working on their own. It will require consortia to come together to share intelligence, identify promising investment options, pool resources, spread risk, improve practice, and reduce transaction costs. Some promising signs of such developments are already in view. One intriguing example is the West Coast's TONIIC consortium, a group of social-impact investors that has come together for precisely this set of purposes.[13] Still, some of the infrastructure identified by the Monitor Institute in 2009 as needed to actualize the promise of impact investing, such as a series of "industry-defining funds that can serve as beacons for how to address specific social or environmental issues," or the placement of substantial risk capital in "catalytic funding structures" that would be available to help incentivize a range of impact investments, have either not yet appeared or are still in embryo.[14] Clearly, fully actualizing the promise of the new frontiers of philanthropy remains a work in progress, though a work that continues to attract talent and energy.

Conclusion

Enormous challenges confront the global community at the present time. Failed states, international terrorism, global warming, persistent poverty, deforestation, water shortages, ill-health, food shortages, and youth unemployment are just some of the problems that exist.

The new tools and actors examined in this volume are not a panacea for solving these problems. Yet it is hard not to see them as one of the more promising developments in an otherwise dismal scenario of lagging resources and resolve. Though not without their problems, these developments hold the promise of bringing significant new resources into efforts to solve the world's problems of poverty, ill-health, and environmental degradation; of unleashing new energies and new sources of ingenuity for social and environmental problem-solving; of democratizing giving and social problem-solving; and of constructively leveraging new technologies and new attitudes about social responsibility to gain new traction on enduring human problems.

It is perhaps not surprising, therefore, that these developments have even found their way into the consciousness of an aging, now-retired, conservative pope, whose 2009 encyclical, *Caritas in Veritate*, pointedly acknowledged that "the traditionally valid distinction between profit-based companies and non-profit organizations can no longer do full justice to reality, or offer practical direction for the future."[15]

The new frontiers of philanthropy described in this book provide powerful support to this observation. But so, too, do they underline the pope's caution about the need to remain vigilant that the "new composite reality" that is emerging, while not excluding profit, makes sure that profit is used, as Benedict put it, as "a means for achieving human and social ends." This is the hope that the new frontiers of philanthropy holds out for us, and that this book, and its companion volume, seek to advance. At a time of diminished resources and diminished expectations, it is, for better or worse, one of the most promising hopes we have.

Suggested Readings

C. K. Prahalad, *The Fortune at the Bottom of the Pyramid: Eradicating Poverty through Profits* (Philadelphia: Wharton School Publishing, 2004).

Lester M. Salamon, editor. *New Frontiers of Philanthropy: A Guide to the New Actors and Tools Reshaping Global Philanthropy and Social Investment* (New York: Oxford University Press, 2014).

Jessica Freireich and Kathryn Fulton, *Investing for Social and Environmental Impact* (n.p.: Monitor Institute, 2009).

Antony Bugg-Levine and Jed Emerson, *Impact Investing: Transforming How We Make Money While Making a Difference* (San Francisco: Jossey-Bass, 2011).

Lucy Carmody, Benjamin McCarron, Jenny Blinch, and Allison Prevatt, *Impact Investing in Emerging Markets* (Singapore: Responsible Research, 2011).

New Frontiers of Philanthropy
Project Advisory Panel

Frank Altman
President and Chief Executive Officer, Community Reinvestment Fund
Doug Bauer
Executive Director, The Clark Foundation
Shari Berenbach
President and Chief Executive Officer, US African Development Foundation
Lucy Bernholz
Founder and President (*former*), Blueprint Research & Design
Stuart Davidson
Managing Partner, Labrador Ventures
Christopher L. Davis
President, Money Management Institute
William Dietel
Managing Partner, Dietel Partners
David Erickson
Director, Center for Community Development Investments, Federal Reserve
Bank of San Francisco
Marc J. Lane
Founder, Marc J. Lane Wealth Group
Maximilian Martin
Founder and Global Managing Director, Impact Economy
Clara Miller
President, F.B. Heron Foundation
Mario Morino
Cofounder and Chairman, Venture Philanthropy Partners
Luther Ragin Jr.
President and Chief Executive Officer, Global Impact Investing Network

Lisa Richter
Principal, GPS Capital Partners
Jack Sim
Founder, World Toilet Organization
Greg Stanton
Founder, Wall Street Without Walls
Vince Stehle
Executive Director, Media Impact Funders
Luc Tayart De Borms
Managing Director, King Baudoin Foundation
Mechai Viravaidya
Founder, Condoms & Cabbages
Kimberly Wright-Violich
President (*former*), Schwab Charitable Fund

Appendix B

Companion Volume

New Frontiers of Philanthropy: A Guide to the New Actors and Tools Reshaping Global Philanthropy and Social Investing

Lester M. Salamon, Editor
Oxford University Press, 2014
ISBN 978019935754

TABLE OF CONTENTS

Notes

Chapter 1

1. "USAID and Impact Investors Capitalize New Equity Fund for East African Agribusiness," Microfinance Africa, accessed May 11, 2013, http://seedstock.com/2011/10/05/usaid-global-impact-investing-network-join-to-create-east-africa-agricultural-investment-fund/.
2. For a discussion of this term in the context of social-impact investing, see Jessica Freireich and Kathryn Fulton, *Investing for Social and Environmental Impact* (n.p.: Monitor Institute, 2009), 33. (Cited hereafter as *2009 Monitor Report.*)
3. For a fuller explication of this nontraditional mode of charitable foundation operation and some of the institutions pioneering it, see Chapter 2 of this volume and Chapter 5 of the companion to this volume, *New Frontiers of Philanthropy: A Guide to the New Actors and Tools Reshaping Global Philanthropy and Social Investing.* Edited by Lester M. Salamon (New York: Oxford University Press, 2014).
4. Cited in John Tzetzes, *Book of Histories (Chiliades)*, trans. Francis R. Walton (Lipsiae, 1826), 2:129–30.
5. For comparison purposes, the assets held by US foundations as of 2010 totaled $618 billion, which yielded approximately $45 billion of charitable grants. By comparison, the assets in commercial banks in the US totaled $14.4 trillion (nearly 25 times the foundation assets), in mutual funds $8.0 trillion, in insurance companies $6.6 trillion, and in money market funds $2.8 trillion. By "leverage" here I do not mean loading mountains of debt on the balance sheets of charities, but rather using charitable resources to stimulate a greater flow of private investment capital into social and environmental purposes. The recent financial crisis is full of lessons about the dangers of over-leveraging, but the philanthropic world is seriously under-leveraged, which brings its own dangers in terms of leaving serious social and environmental problems to fester. Foundation data from the Foundation Center accessed at Foundation Center, "Highlights of Foundation Yearbook," *Foundations Today Series* (2011), accessed May 10, 2013, http://foundation-center.org/gainknowledge/research/pdf/fy2011_highlights.pdf; data on other institutions from the Federal Reserve as reported in the US Census Bureau, *Statistical Abstract of the United States, 2012*, accessed May 10, 2013, http://www.census.gov/compendia/statab/cats/banking_finance_insurance/financial_assets_and_liabilities.html.
6. Based on data generated by the International Association of Microfinance Investors, "Microfinance Investment," International Association of Microfinance Investors, accessed May 11, 2013, http://www.iamfi.com/microfinance_investment.html.

7. "About Us," Aavishkaar, accessed August 12, 2012, http://www.aavishkaar.in.

8. Grassroots Business Fund, *2011 Annual Report of the Grassroots Business Fund* (Washington, DC: Grassroots Business Fund, 2011), accessed May 11, 2013, http://gbfund.org/sites/default/files/GBF_AR_2011.pdf.

9. "The Bamboo Finance Private Equity Group," Bamboo Finance, accessed May 11, 2013, www.bamboofinance.com.

10. Small Enterprise Assistance Fund (SEAF), "Our Impact," accessed June 6, 2013, http://seaf.com/index.php?option=com_content&view=article&id=36&Itemid=82&lang=en.

11. C. K. Prahalad, *The Fortune at the Bottom of the Pyramid: Eradicating Poverty through Profits* (Philadelphia: Wharton School Publishing, 2004).

12. Lucy Carmody, Benjamin McCarron, Jenny Blinch, and Allison Prevatt, *Impact Investing in Emerging Markets* (Singapore: Responsible Research, 2011), 102.

13. On some of the difficulties of the "impact investment" terminology, see below and Chapter 20 of the companion volume.

14. Antony Bugg-Levine and Jed Emerson, *Impact Investing: Transforming How We Make Money While Making a Difference* (San Francisco: Jossey-Bass, 2011), 151.

15. Lester M. Salamon, ed., *New Frontiers of Philanthropy: A Guide to the New Tools and Actors Reshaping Global Philanthropy and Social Investing* (New York: Oxford University Press, 2014). ISBN: 9780199357543. See Appendix B for a full table of contents and ordering information.

16. Christa Velasquez, "Advancing Social Impact Investment through Measurement," accessed May 11, 2013, http://www.frbsf.org/cdinvestments/conferences/social impact-investments/transcript/Velasquez_Panel_3.pdf.

17. As noted more fully below, the term "philanthrocapitalism" was coined by Matthew Bishop and Michael Green to depict a new class of dot-com billionaires like Bill Gates who have turned their attention to philanthropy. See Matthew Bishop and Michael Green, *Philanthrocapitalism: How the Rich Can Save the World* (New York: Bloomsbury, 2008). The terms "impact investment" and "impact investors" were coined by a group of philanthropists and investors assembled by the Rockefeller Foundation to consider how to expand the available pool of resources for social- and environmental-purpose activities.

18. This definition is consistent with *Webster's New World Dictionary*, which defines "philanthropy" as "a desire to help mankind"; and "philanthropic" as "interest in the general human welfare." Victoria Neufeldt, *Webster's New World Dictionary of American English, Third College Edition* (New York: Prentice Hall, 1991), 1014.

19. *Webster's New World Dictionary, Third College Edition*, 1272.

20. Frieriech and Fulton, *2009 Monitor Report*, 6.

21. Nick O'Donohoe, Christina Leijonhufvud, Yasemin Saltuk, Antony Bugg-Levine, and Margot Brandenburg, *Impact Investments: An Emerging Asset Class* (New York: J.P. Morgan, 2010), 5.

22. Bugg-Levine and Emerson, *Impact Investing*, 9.

23. Steven Godeke and Raúl Pomares with Albert V. Bruno, Pat Guerra, Charly Kleisner, and Hersh Shefrin, *Solutions for Impact Investors: From Strategy to Implementation* (New York: Rockefeller Philanthropy Advisors, 2009), 10.

24. Bugg-Levine and Emerson, *Impact Investing*, 9.

25. Freireich and Fulton, *2009 Monitor Report*, 35–36.

26. Kevin Starr, "The Trouble with Impact Investing: P1," *Stanford Social Investment Review* (January 24, 2012): 22, accessed May 11, 2013, http://www.ssireview.org/blog/entry/the_trouble_with_impact_investing_part_1.

27. In a lead article in a recent edition of the Federal Reserve Bank of San Francisco's *Community Development Investment Review*, Thornley and Dailey thus call attention to their use of the term "community impact investing" rather than "impact investing" precisely in order to make clear that they are focusing on "low-income domestic markets and only to investments targeting social returns." Ben Thornley and Colby Dailey, "Building Scale in Community Impact Investing through Nonfinancial Performance Measurement," *Community Development Investment Review* 6.1 (2010): 3.

28. Bugg-Levine and Emerson, *Impact Investing*, xix.

29. This usage is also gaining ground in international circles. Thus, for example, the UK's new Big Society Capital institution refers to its field of activity as "social investment," which it defines as "the provision and use of capital to generate social as well as financial returns." See "Social Investment Is a Way of Using Capital to Generate Social Impact as well as Some Financial Return for Investors," Big Society Capital, accessed May 11, 2013, http://www.bigsocietycapital.com/what-social-investment.

30. For the former position see, for example, Rob Schwartz, *Social Investment* (London: Clearly So, 2012). For the latter position see Freireich and Fulton, *2009 Monitor Report*, 14.

31. In the US, the breakdown of these sources for the core nonprofit service and expressive organizations takes the following form: 10 percent from private philanthropy from all sources; 38 percent from government grants and payments; and 52 percent from private fees and payments. See Lester M. Salamon, *America's Nonprofit Sector: A Primer*, 3rd ed. (New York: Foundation Center, 2012), 39.

32. Lester M. Salamon and Stephanie Geller, "Investment Capital: The New Challenge for American Nonprofits," *Communiqué* 5 (Baltimore: Johns Hopkins Nonprofit Listening Post Project, 2006), 5, http://ccss.jhu.edu/publications-findings?did=265.

33. Salamon and Geller, "Investment Capital," 8.

Chapter 2

1. Included here were the Kentucky Highlands Investment Corporation (1968), the Massachusetts Capital Resource Company (1977), the Arkansas Capital Corporation (1985), and Kansas Venture Capital, Inc. (1987), See "Kentucky Highlands Investment Corporation," Rural Housing and Economic Development Gateway, US Department of Housing and Urban Development, accessed March 2, 2013, http://www.hud.gov/offices/cpd/economicdevelopment/programs/rhed/gateway/pdf/KentuckyHighlands.pdf; "Mass Capital, Company," Massachusetts Capital Resource Company, accessed May 11, 2013, http://www.masscapital.com/company/; "Company History & Information," Arkansas Capital Corporation Group, accessed May 11, 2013, http://arcapital.com/programs/our-history/; "Kansas Venture Capital, Inc. ("KVCI")," Kansas Venture Capital, Inc., accessed May 11, 2013, http://www.kvci.com/. I am indebted to Belden Daniels for references to these early entities.

2. These included programs such as the following: the Low-Income Housing Tax Credit, which provides tax incentives for private investments in low-income housing; the 1977

Community Reinvestment Act, which made regulatory decisions on bank branching contingent on demonstrations by banks that they were making investments in the same low-income neighborhoods from which they were extracting deposits; and tax and grant subsidies for so-called community development finance institutions, i.e., financial institutions with a primary mission of improving economic conditions for low-income individuals and communities. For more detailed discussions of these developments, see David Erickson, *The Housing Policy Revolution* (Washington, DC: Urban Institute Press, 2008); and Lean Benjamin, Julia Sass Rubin, and Sean Zielenbach, "Community Development Financial Institutions: Expanding Access to Capital in Under-served Markets," in *The Community Development Reader*, ed. James DeFilippis and Susan Saegert (New York: Routledge, 2008).

3. For a discussion of "impact investing" as an "asset class," see O'Donohoe et al., *Impact Investments*, 6.

4. CGAP, "The History of Microfinance," prepared for CGAP UNCDF donor training, "The New Vision of Microfinance: Financial Services for the Poor," accessed June 11, 2013, http://www.slideshare.net/JosephSam/the-history-of-microfinance-cgap. Cited in Lisa Richter, "Capital Aggregators," Chapter 2 in Salamon, *New Frontiers of Philanthropy*.

5. "CDFI Data Project," Opportunity Finance Network, accessed February 13, 2014, http://www.opportunityfinance.net/industry/default.aspx?id=234; see also O'Donohoe et al., *Impact Investments*, 80–81.

6. These concepts were first articulated by Freireich and Fulton, *2009 Monitor Report*, 32. See also Thornley and Dailey, "Nonfinancial Performance Measurement," 6.

7. This figure is adapted from one presented in Freireich and Fulton, *2009 Monitor Report*, 32. However, Freireich and Fulton assume that all social-impact investors have the same financial and social-impact expectations. In fact, however, there is reason to question this assumption, though the basic concept that some meaningful floor exists for both social and financial return for both sets of investors, and the many that fall in between, is a crucial defining one for the field.

8. "About Us," Acumen Fund, accessed August 18, 2012, http://acumen.org/.

9. Willow Impact Investors, for example, describes itself as pursuing "an investment strategy that seeks to generate market-rate returns or more, while investing in businesses that deliver tangible positive environmental impact or social benefit." The firm identifies as its "primary objective" to "deliver strong and sustainable financial returns for our investors while achieving maximum social and environmental impact." "Investment Policy," Willow Impact Investors, accessed March 2, 2013, http://www.willowimpact.com/about-us/company/investment-policy.html.

10. Adam Gromis, Impact Exchange Manager, e-mail to author, September 4, 2012. See also Jasmin Saltuk, Amit Bouri, and Giselle Leung, *Insight into the Impact Investment Market: An In-Depth Analysis of Investor Perspectives and over 2,200 Transactions* (London: J.P. Morgan Social Investment, 2011), 8.

11. Richter, "Capital Aggregators."

12. "Global Trends in Clean Energy Investment: Q4 2009 Clean Energy Fact Pack," New Energy Finance, accessed May 11, 2013, http://www.newenergyfinance.com.

13. O'Donohue et al., *Impact Investments*, 6.

14. Carmody et al., *Impact Investing in Emerging Markets*, 10; O'Donohoe et al., *Impact Investments*, 34–35; Saltuk, Bouri, and Leung, *Impact Investment Market*, 24–27.

15. For a discussion of the tool of "securitization," see Chapter 14 by Mary Tingerthal in Salamon, *New Frontiers of Philanthropy.*

16. David J. Erickson, "Secondary Markets," Chapter 3 in Salamon, *New Frontiers of Philanthropy.*

17. "Quick Facts," Community Reinvestment Fund, accessed September 1, 2012, http://www.crfusa.com/AboutCRF/Pages/QuickFacts.aspx.

18. "Flexible Capital Access Program (FlexCap): Investment Summary," Habitat for Humanity International, accessed May 11, 2013, https://www.missioninvestors.org/system/files/tools/Habitat%20for%20Humanity%27s%20FlexCAP%20summary.pdf.

19. "Fact Sheet," Blue Orchard, accessed May 11, 2013, http://www.blueorchard.com/jahia/webdav/site/blueorchard/shared/Publications%20and%20Resources/BlueOrchard%20Factsheets/0907_Fact%20sheet%202009_EN.pdf.

20. Durreen Shahnaz and Robert Kraybill, "Social and Environmental Exchanges," Chapter 4 in Salamon, *New Frontiers of Philanthropy.*

21. World Bank, *State and Trends of the Carbon Market* (Washington, DC: World Bank Group, 2011), 9, accessed May 11, 2013, http://siteresources.worldbank.org/intcarbonfinance/Resources. For a discussion of recent trends, including a 2013 refusal by the European Parliament to support a slowdown in the issuance of new permits in view of the drop in their price, see Stanley Reed and Mark Scott, "In Europe, Paid Permits for Pollution Are Fizzling," *New York Times*, April 22, 2013, B1.

22. Evan Weaver, "Marrying Cash and Change: Social 'Stock Markets' Spread Worldwide," *Christian Science Monitor*, August 30, 2012, accessed November 15, 2013, http://www.csmonitor.com/World/Making-a-difference/Change-Agent/2012/0830/Marrying-cash-and-change-Social-stock-markets-spread-worldwide.

23. Carmody et al., *Impact Investing in Emerging Markets*, 60.

24. "The IDB Group: Your Partner for Impact Investing in Latin America and the Caribbean," IDB Group, accessed May 11, 2012, http://idbdocs.iadb.org/wsdocs/getdocument.aspx?docnum=36886146.

25. "About Us," NESTA, accessed May 11, 2013, http://www.nesta.org.uk/about_us; Robert Hutton, "Cameron Opens $1 Billion Big Society Bank to Fund Charities," Bloomberg, April 4, 2012, accessed May 11, 2013, http://www.bloomberg.com/news/2012-04-03/cameron-opens-1-billion-big-society-bank-to-fund-charities.html; "How We Are Funded," Big Society Capital, accessed May 11, 2013, http://www.bigsocietycapital.com/how-we-are-funded.

26. One recent estimate puts the amount of foundation assets subjected to such screens at some $60 billion in the US, roughly 10 percent of all foundation assets, still a fairly small fraction of total foundation assets, but growing. US SIF, Forum for Sustainable and Responsible Investment, *Report on Sustainable and Responsible Investing Trends in the United States: 2012* (Washington, DC: US SIF, 2012), 54. For more detail on such "socially responsible investing," see Chapter 18 of the companion volume.

27. In the US, for example, foundations are required by law to dispense at least 5 percent of the value of their assets in grants or related administrative costs in support of their approved charitable missions

28. Lester M. Salamon and William E. Burckart, "Foundations as Philanthropic Banks," Chapter 5 in Salamon, *New Frontiers of Philanthropy.*

29. I am indebted to Thomas van Dyke and Shari Berenbach for identification of a number of these institutions.

30. Data on the number of foundations making PRIs and the share of qualifying distributions recently taking this form from Steven Lawrence, "Doing Good with Foundation Assets: An Updated Look at Program-Related Investments," in *The PRI Directory*, 3rd ed., ed. Foundation Center (New York: Foundation Center, 2010), xiii. Total number of private foundations in the US from Foundation Center, *Foundation Yearbook* (New York: Foundation Center, 2010). In an effort to promote greater use of the PRI mechanism, the Internal Revenue Service recently issued a proposed rule that would provide a broader array of examples of the types of activities that would satisfy the IRS restrictions on PRIs. Internal Revenue Service, "Notice of Proposed Rulemaking: Examples of Program-Related Investments REG-144267-11," in *Internal Revenue Bulletin: 2012-21*, May 21, 2012, accessed April 13, 2013, http://www.irs.gov/irb/2012-21_IRB/ar11.html.

31. Lisa Hagerman and David Woods," Enterprise Brokers," Chapter 6 in Salamon, *New Frontiers of Philanthropy.*

32. For further detail on these "new capacity builders," see Melinda Tuan, "Capacity Builders and Venture Philanthropy," Chapter 7 in Salamon, *New Frontiers of Philanthropy.*

33. Christine Letts, William Ryan, and Allen Grossman, "Virtuous Capital: What Foundations Can Learn from Venture Capitalists," *Harvard Business Review* (March–April 1997): 36–46.

34. Edna McConnell Clark Foundation "How We Work," accessed May 11, 2013, http://www.emcf.org/how-we-work/.

35. "About Us," New Profit, accessed May 11, 2013, http://newprofit.com/cgi-bin/iowa/about/9.html.

36. European Venture Philanthropy Association, *European Venture Philanthropy Directory 2010/11* (Brussels: European Venture Philanthropy Association, 2010), 15. Unlike their US counterparts, European venture philanthropy organizations combine the attributes of US venture philanthropies, which generally restrict themselves to grant funding, with what we have termed "foundations as philanthropic banks," which deploy a far wider array of financial instruments.

37. "About," The Hub, accessed October 20, 2012, http://www.the-hub.net/about.

38. "About," Opportunity Finance Network, accessed October 12, 2012, www.opportunityfinance.net/about.

39. "About Us," UN PRI, accessed October 20, 2012, http://www.unpri.org; "About Us," Social Investment Forum, accessed October 20, 2012, http://www.socialinvest.org.

40. "About Us," CGAP, accessed October 20, 2012, http://www.cgap.org/p/site/c/aboutus/.

41. "What's New in Mission Investing," Mission Investors Exchange, accessed October 20, 2012, http://www.moreformission.org; "About Mission Investors Exchange," Mission Investors Exchange, accessed October 20, 2012, https://www.missioninvestors.org/about-us; "The Origins of Mission Investors Exchange," Mission Investors Exchange, accessed October 20, 2012, http://www.missioninvestors.org/about-us/origins-mission-investors-exchange.

42. Freireich and Fulton, *2009 Monitor Report*, 12.

43. O'Donohoe et al., *Impact Investments*, 17.

44. For further detail on these entities, see Vince Stehle, "On-Line Portals and Exchanges," Chapter 8 in Salamon, *New Frontiers of Philanthropy.*

45. Markets for Good, *Upgrading the Information Infrastructure for Social Change* (Summer 2012), 11, accessed May 11, 2013, http://www.marketsforgood.org/wordpress/wp-content/uploads/2012/11/MarketsforGood_Information-Infrastructure_Fall-2012_.pdf.

46. "About," Kiva, accessed October 20, 2012, http://www.kiva.org/about/stats.

47. "TechSoup Global by the Numbers, Quarterly Report, October 2010, " TechSoupGlobal, accessed May 11, 2013, http://www.techsoupglobal.org/press/selectcoverage.

48. "Our 2011 Annual Report Infographic," VolunteerMatch, accessed October 23, 2012, http://blogs.volunteermatch.org/engagingvolunteers/2012/06/25/our-2011-annual-report-infographic-the-story-of-you/.

49. For further detail on these entities, see Rick Cohen, "Corporate-Originated Charitable Funds," Chapter 9 in Salamon, *New Frontiers of Philanthropy*.

50. "2011 Donor-Advised Fund Report," National Philanthropic Trust, accessed May 11, 2013, http://www.nptrust.org/images/uploads/2011%20Donor-Advised-Fund-Report%281%29.pdf.

51. Early critiques of the corporate-originated charitable funds centered on the fact that they were legally constituted as "public charities" as opposed to foundations, and thereby avoided the legal restrictions on foundations, including the restrictions requiring the payout of at least 5 percent of their assets each year as grants. As Cohen shows, however, the larger such funds have established internal procedures that encourage robust payout, and most of the funds have proved to have payout rates at least as high as those required of foundations.

52. This discussion draws heavily on Lester M. Salamon, "Privatization for the Social Good: A New Avenue for Global Foundation-Building," in *The Privatization Barometer* (July 2010), 48–54; and Lester M. Salamon, *Philanthropication thru Privatization: Building Assets for Social Progress* (New York: East-West Management Institute, 2013). Available at http://bit.ly/1brWDcL.

53. Examples of these other foundations include Deutsche Bundesstiftung Umwelt, Landesstiftung Baden-Wurtemberg, and Stiftung Innovation (Rhineland-Palatinate).

54. Salamon, *Philanthropication thru Privatization*.

55. In 1990, for example, Italy converted its 88 small, nonprofit, and quasi-public savings banks into joint stock companies, but left the ownership of the resulting stock in a set of what became 88 foundations, which inherited the charitable arms of the preexisting savings banks. Thanks to a number of strategic consolidations and mergers among the owned banks, by the time the foundations were authorized to sell this stock in 1994, its value exceeded €24 billion (or US$31 billion at current exchange rates). Since then the assets of these "foundations of banking origin" have climbed further, producing a philanthropic revolution that has transformed Italy from a philanthropic backwater into one of the leading philanthropic nations in the world as measured by the per capita size of its philanthropic endowments. As of 2008, the combined assets of Italy's foundations of banking origin exceeded €50 billion, or some US$65 billion. Fondazione Cariplo and Compagnia di San Paolo, two of the largest of these foundations, both had assets in excess of €9 billion, or approximately US$12 billion, as of 2008, which put both of them ahead of such major US foundations as the Rockefeller Foundation ($3.1 billion in assets as of 2008), and the Ford Foundation, America's second largest ($9.1 billion in assets as of 2008). Data on US foundations from Foundation Center, *Foundation Yearbook: Facts and Figures on Private and Community Foundations, 2008 Edition* (New York: Foundation

Center, 2008), 18. Data on Ford Foundation: "About," Ford Foundation, accessed February 6, 2010, http://www.fordfound.org/about.

A virtually identical process occurred even earlier in New Zealand, when a series of New Zealand nonprofit savings banks were converted into stock companies, and the shares placed into a network of 12 community trusts. More recently, the purchase of a number of nonprofit health insurance organizations and hospitals by for-profit firms in the US has led to the creation of close to 200 so-called health conversion foundations, including the $3.3 billion California Endowment. For further detail see Grantmakers in Health, "A Profile of Foundations Created from Health Care Conversions," 2009, accessed November 15, 2013, http://www.gih.org/files/usrdoc/2009_Conversion_Report.pdf.

56. For further detail on these funding collaboratives, see Angela Eikenberry and Jessica Bearman, "Funding Collaboratives," Chapter 10 in Salamon, *New Frontiers of Philanthropy.*

57. "Global Gathering," TONIIC, accessed October 19, 2012, http://toniicglobalgathering.eventbrite.com/.

58. "History," Living Cities, accessed October 19, 2012, http://www.livingcities.org/about/history/.

59. "About," Angel Investors Network, accessed October 19, 2012, http://www.angelinvestors.net/about.

Chapter 3

1. For an analysis of the use of varied tools of action, including varied financial tools of action, in the governmental sphere, see Lester M. Salamon, *The Tools of Government: A Guide to the New Governance* (New York: Oxford University Press, 2002).

2. Lawrence, "Doing Good," xvi.

3. Sarah Cooch and Mark Kramer, "Compounding Impact: Mission Investing by US Foundations," FSG Social Impact Advisors, 2007, 17, accessed November 15, 2013, http://www.cdfifund.gov/what_we_do/resources/Compounding%20Impact%20Mission%20Investing%20by%20US%20Foundations.pdf.

4. Saltuk, Bouri, and Leung, *Impact Investment Market,* 11–12. Two years later, however, this same source reported that the share of impact investors surveyed who reported using a private equity instrument exceeded the share reporting use of debt by 83 percent to 66 percent, though no information was provided on the numbers of transactions of each type that these different investors made. See Yasemin Saltuk, Amit Bouri, Abhilash Mudaliar, and Min Pease, *Perspectives on Progress: The Impact Investor Survey* (London: J.P. Morgan Social Finance, January 2013), 9.

5. For further detail on the character and operation of loans and credit enhancements, see Norah McVeigh and Julia Sass Rubin, "Loans, Loan Guarantees, and Credit Enhancements," Chapter 12 in Salamon, *New Frontiers of Philanthropy.*

6. "USAID, Global Impact Investing Network Join to Create East Africa Agricultural Investment Fund," SeedStock, accessed May 11, 2013, http://seedstock.com/2011/10/05/usaid-global-impact-investing-network-join-to-create-east-africa-agricultural-investment-fund/.

7. For further detail, see Alex Nichols and Rod Schwartz, "The Demand Side of the Philanthropic Marketplace," Chapter 21 in Salamon, *New Frontiers of Philanthropy.*

8. Financial Markets Series, *Bond Markets 2011* (London: TheCityUK, 2011), 1, accessed May 11, 2013, http://www.thecityuk.com/assets/Uploads/BondMarkets2011.pdf.

9. For further detail on the operation and use of bonds in social-impact investing, see Shari Berenbach and Elise Balboni, "Fixed-Income Securities," Chapter 13 in Salamon, *New Frontiers of Philanthropy*.

10. "Bonds," IFFIm, accessed May 11, 2013, http://www.iffim.org/bonds/.

11. "Community Investment Note," Calvert Foundation, accessed May 11, 2013, http://www.calvertfoundation.org/invest/how-to-invest/community-investment-note.

12. Some securitization transactions use a financial instrument called a collateralized debt obligation (CDO) instead of a bond as the vehicle for raising capital from investors. CDOs can be backed by a variety of types of loans and can be sold in "tranches" that carry different maturities, interest rates, and risk associated with them. For further detail on securitization in the social-purpose arena, see Tingerthal, "Securitization," in Salamon, *New Frontiers of Philanthropy*.

13. For further detail on equity and quasi-equity, see Monica Brand and John Kohler, "Private Equity Investments," Chapter 15 in Salamon, *New Frontiers of Philanthropy*.

14. Cooch and Kramer, *Compounding Impact*, 17. A later study of 74 mission-investing foundations by the Foundation Center found half of these institutions making mission-related equity investments, but mostly in publicly traded equities, though a third reported making private equity investments of the sort typically available to small, social enterprises. Steven Lawrence and Reina Mukai, *Key Facts on Mission Investing* (New York: Foundation Center, 2011), 3.

15. Saltuk, Bouri, and Leung, *Impact Investment Market*, 11.

16. Saltuk et al., *Perspectives on Progress*, 9.

17. Joshua Humphreys, "Sustainability Trends in US Alternative Investment," US SIF Foundation: Forum for Sustainable and Responsible Investment, 2011, 3, accessed October 19, 2012, http://www.investorscircle.net/accelsite/media/3195/Sustainability%20Trends%20in%20US%20Alternative%20Investments%20Report.pdf.

18. This set of venture capital funds is supported by a trade association called the Community Development Venture Capital Alliance (CDVCA).

19. "Equity Investments," Kentucky Highlands Investment Corporation, accessed November 3, 2012, http://www.khic.org/equity.html. Another example of the same type of fund is CEI Ventures, a for-profit subsidiary of a 26-year-old community development financial institution headquartered in Wiscasset, Maine, that makes equity investments in promising companies providing quality jobs for low-income people in northern New England. The firm's Coastal Ventures II fund raised $20 million from 30 institutional and individual investors for equity investments in companies that "promote socially beneficial products and services, opportunities for women and minorities, environmentally friendly business practices, and the enrichment of distressed and rural communities." "Overview," CEI Ventures, accessed November 3, 2012, http://www.ceiventures.com/.

20. "About Us," Aavishkaar, accessed November 4, 2012, http://www.aavishkaar.in/about-us/.

21. Humphreys, "US Alternative Investment."

22. For a discussion of these and other features of equity investing, see Monica Brand and John Kohler, "Private Equity Investments," Chapter 15 in Salamon, *New Frontiers of Philanthropy*.

23. For a fuller discussion of the tool of "socially responsible investing and purchasing," see Steve Lydenberg and Katie Grace, "Socially Responsible Investing and Purchasing," Chapter 18 in Salamon, *New Frontiers of Philanthropy*.

24. US Social Investment Forum Foundation, *Sustainable and Responsible Investing Trends*, 11; Eurosif, *European SRI Study: 2012* (Brussels: Eurosif, 2012), 63, accessed May 11, 2013, http://www.eurosif.org/research/eurosif-sri-study/sri-study-2012.

25. Social Enterprise UK, *Fightback Britain: A Report on the State of Social Enterprise Survey 2011* (London: Social Enterprise UK, 2011), 15.

26. A "matched bargain market" is a private trading platform, typically handled by an investment company, through which social-purpose investors can sell their shares to other investors looking to enter a particular market. One example is that provided by the Ethical Property Company (EPC) in the UK. This social venture offers office space for social-purpose organizations in the UK. It finances its property acquisitions from equity capital raised from the sale of shares. Its shares are not sold on the London Stock Exchange or the Alternative Investment Market, however. Rather, its 1,357 shareholders bought their shares through a matched bargain market guided by Stocktrade, a division of the stockbroker firm of Brewin Dolphin, which also handles all trades and is responsible for using all reasonable effort to match willing buyers and sellers both for EPC and other social ventures that have chosen to use this route to financing their operations as well. "How to Invest," Ethical Property, accessed November 4, 2012, http://www.ethicalproperty.co.uk/howtoinvest.php.

27. "Investment Approach," Aavishkaar, accessed November 4, 2012, http://www.aavishkaar.in/about-us/investment-approach/.

28. For further detail on "quasi-equity," see Brand and Kohler, "Private Equity Investments," in Salamon, *New Frontiers of Philanthropy*.

29. For information on the HCT Group, see "Welcome to HCT Group," HCT Group, accessed November 4, 2012, http://www.hctgroup.org.

30. For further detail on social-impact bonds or "pay for success," see Drew van Glahn and Caroline Whistler, "Social Impact Bonds / Pay-for-Success," Chapter 16 in Salamon, *New Frontiers of Philanthropy*.

31. The goal is to reduce the 60 percent recidivism rate for such offenders and thereby save the government millions of pounds. If the funded social sector organizations providing the wraparound rehabilitation services succeed in reducing one-year postrelease reconvictions by at least 7.5 percent among this population compared to a control group, then the investors will get their money back with 2.5 percent interest. If the performance exceeds this target, investors will be rewarded with a return higher than this, up to a maximum of 13 percent. Based on information available in Social Finance, *A New Tool for Scaling Impact: How Social Impact Bonds Can Mobilize Private Capital to Advance Social Good* (Boston: Social Finance, 2012), accessed November 4, 2012, http://www.socialfinance.org.uk/resources/social-finance/new-tool-scaling-impact-how-social impact-bonds-can-mobilize-private-capita; "Home," Social Finance, accessed November 4, 2012, http://www.socialfinance.org.uk

32. MDRC, a New York–based employment and training organization, will manage the program and make payments to a set of nonprofit organizations that will carry out the program. For Goldman Sachs to break even on its payments to MDRC, the program will have to reduce recidivism on the part of program participants by 10 percent compared to a control group. Greater success will save the city more money and accrue a higher

return for Goldman Sachs. "Mayor Bloomberg, Deputy Mayor Gibbs, and Corrections Commissioner Schriro Announce the Nation's First Social Impact Bond Program," City of New York, Office of the Mayor, accessed November 4, 2012, http://www.nyc.gov/html/index.html.

33. Jim Roth, Denis Garand, and Stuart Rutherford, *The Landscape of Microinsurance in the World's 100 Poorest Countries* (Appleton, WI: Microinsurance Center, 2007).

34. On the International Labour Organization's Microinsurance Innovation Facility, see "Microinsurance Innovation Facility," International Labour Organization, accessed May 11, 2013, www.ilo.org/microinsurance. For a broader discussion of microinsurance, see Chapter 17, "Insurance," by Craig Churchill and Lauren Peterson, in Salamon, *New Frontiers of Philanthropy*.

35. Swiss Reinsurance Company, *Microinsurance—Risk Protection for 4 Billion People* (Zurich: Swiss Re, 2010); Craig Churchill and Michael J. McCord, "Emerging Trends in Microinsurance," in *Protecting the Poor: A Microinsurance Compendium*, vol. 2, ed. Craig Churchill and Michal Matul (Geneva: International Labor Organization and Munich Re Foundation, 2012).

36. For a discussion of this and other innovations mentioned here, see Churchill and Matul, *Protecting the Poor.*

37. For further detail on these initiatives, see Chapter 17 in Salamon, *New Frontiers of Philanthropy.*

38. O'Donohoe et al., *Impact Investments*, 5.

39. For further detail on these approaches, see Lydenberg and Grace, "Socially Responsible Investing and Purchasing," in Salamon, *New Frontiers of Philanthropy.*

40. Eurosif, *European SRI Study*, 63, The seven distinct types of socially responsible investment mechanism identified by Eurosif include sustainability-themed investment, best-in-class investment selection, norms-based screening, exclusion of holdings from investment universe, integration of ESG factors in financial analysis, engagement and voting on sustainability matters, and impact investment.

41. Eurosif, *European SRI Study*, 7.

42. Quoted in Lester M. Salamon, *Rethinking Corporate Social Engagement: Lessons from Latin America* (Sterling, VA: Kumarian Press, 2010), 33.

43. See, for example, David Vogel, *The Market for Virtue: The Potential and Limits of Corporate Social Responsibility* (Washington, DC: Brookings Institution Press, 2005), 37.

44. The discussion here draws heavily on Peter Frumkin, "Grants," Chapter 19 in Salamon, *New Frontiers of Philanthropy.*

45. McKinsey and Company, *And the Winner Is…Capturing the Promise of Philanthropic Prizes* (n.p.: McKinsey and Co., 2009), 16.

Chapter 4

1. Lester Brown, *World on Edge: How to Prevent Environmental and Economic Collapse* (New York: W.W. Norton, 2011).

2. Brown, *World on Edge*, PowerPoint presentation available at "Books," Earth Policy Institute, accessed April 14, 2013, http://www.earth-policy.org/books/wote.

3. Landon Thomas, Jr., "As the Bailouts Continue in Europe, So Does the Flouting of Rules," *New York Times*, November 29, 2012, B3.

4. David Jolly and Jack Ewing, "Unemployment in Euro Zone Reaches New High," *New York Times,* November 30, 2012, accessed May 11, 2013, http://www.nytimes.com/2012/12/01/business/global/daily-euro-zone-watch.html.

5. Salamon, *America's Nonprofit Sector,* 39.

6. David Bornstein, *How to Change the World: Social Entrepreneurs and the Power of New Ideas* (New York: Oxford University Press, 2004), 1.

7. Lester M. Salamon, "The Rise of the Nonprofit Sector," *Foreign Affairs* 73.4 (July–August, 1994): 109–22.

8. See Bornstein, *How to Change the World,* for examples of such actors. On the "global associational revolution," see Salamon, "The Rise of the Nonprofit Sector."

9. See, for example: Carlos Borzaga and Jacques Defourny, *The Emergence of Social Enterprise* (London: Routledge, 2001); Alex Nichols, *Social Entrepreneurship: New Models of Sustainable Social Change* (Oxford: Oxford University Press, 2006); Dennis R. Young, Lester M. Salamon, and Mary Clark Grinsfelder, "Commercialization, Social Ventures, and For-Profit Competition," in *The State of Nonprofit America,* 2nd ed., ed. Lester M. Salamon (Washington, DC: Brookings Institution Press, 2012).

10. Peer Stein, Tony Goland, and Robert Schiff, *Two Trillion and Counting: Assessing the Credit Gap for Micro, Small, and Medium-Size Enterprises in the Developing World* (n.p: International Finance Corporation and McKinsey & Company, 2010), 1.

11. O'Donohoe et al., *Impact Investments,* 39.

12. Although, only three-tenths of 1 percent of all foundations—less than 200 institutions in all out of more than 75,000—have made any PRI in a typical recent year, and only eight-tenths of 1 percent of foundation charitable distributions are taking this form, the fact remains that the PRI program created a significant cadre of foundations skilled in making charitable investments in low-income housing, community development, minority housing, and other social-purpose activities. Data on the number of foundations making PRIs and the share of qualifying distributions recently taking this form from Lawrence, "Doing Good"," xiii. The total number of private foundations in the US is from Foundation Center, *Foundation Yearbook, 2009* (New York: Foundation Center, 2010). For further description of the revolution in housing policy that these initiatives fostered, see Erickson, *The Housing Policy Revolution.*

13. "Mission and History," Calvert Foundation, accessed January 2, 2013, http://www.calvertfoundation.org/index.php?option=com_content&view=article&id=66&Itemid=76; "Acumen Fund Ten Year Report, 2001–2011," 2011), 1, accessed January 2, 2013, http://www.acumenfund.org/uploads/assets/documents/Acumen%20Fund%20Ten%20Year%20Report%202001%20-%202011a_3wcsNw56.pdf.

14. "About Us," Acumen Fund, accessed December 4, 2012, http://www.acumenfund.org/about-us.html.

15. Prahalad, *Fortune at the Bottom of the Pyramid.*

16. For a fuller portrayal of this model, see Salamon and Burckart, "Foundations as Philanthropic Banks," in Salamon, *New Frontiers of Philanthropy.*

17. Charly and Lisa Kleissner, and Raul Pomares, personal interviews with author, March 26, 2010 and January 23, 2012.

18. Bishop and Green, *Philanthrocapitalism,* 6.

19. Atul Dighe, "Demographic and Technological Imperatives," in Salamon, *State of Nonprofit America*; William Strauss and Neil Howe, *Millennials Rising: The Next Great Generation* (New York: Vantage, 2000).

20. "Home Page," Net Impact, accessed October 1, 2012, http://netimpact.org/.

21. "About Us: Our Team," Willow Impact Investors, accessed August 10, 2012, http://www.willowimpact.com/about-us/.

22. Data on rates from *New York Times*, January 4, 2013, B8. "Battered investor syndrome" comment from Ed Yardeni, founder of Yardeni Research, as quoted in Nathan Popper, "Even with Fiscal Agreement, Investors Facing Imminent Obstacles," *New York Times*, January 1, 2013, accessed September 14, 2013, http://www.nytimes.com/2013/01/02/business/economy/daily-stock-market-activity.html?_r=0.

23. O'Donohoe et al., *Impact Investments*, 11, 31–34; Saltuk, Bouri, and Leung, *Impact Investment Market*, 16–24.

24. "Investing for Social & Environmental Impact: A Design for Catalyzing an Emerging Industry," Monitor Institute, accessed May 11, 2013, http://www.monitorinstitute.com/impactinvesting/documents/InvestingforSocialandEnvImpact_FullReport_004.pdf

25. O'Donohoe et al., *Impact Investments*, 17.

Chapter 5

1. Brian Trelstad, "The Elusive Quest for Impact: The Evolving Practice of Social Impact Measurement," Chapter 22 in Salamon, *New Frontiers of Philanthropy*.

2. "Benefit corporations" are businesses that meet especially demanding standards of corporate purpose, accountability, and transparency. B-Lab provides a rating system for such corporations and awards a "B-corporation" label to companies that demonstrate adherence to one of a number of third-party rating systems for corporations. "About B-lab," B-Lab, accessed February 5, 2013, http://www.benefitcorp.net/about-b-lab.

3. "How GIIRS Works," B-Lab, accessed February 5, 2013, http://www.giirs.org/about-giirs/how-giirs-works.

4. See Lyndenberg and Grace, "Socially Responsible Investing and Purchasing," in Salamon, *New Frontiers of Philanthropy*.

5. O'Donohue et al., *Impact Investments*, 72; E. T. Jackson and Associates, *Accelerating Impact: Achievements, Challenges and What's Next in Building the Impact Investing Industry* (New York: Rockefeller Foundation, 2012), xvi.

6. Thornley and Dailey, "Nonfinancial Performance Measurement," 16.

7. O'Donohue et al., *Impact Investments*, 22. More recent data suggest some improvement in the penetration of nonfinancial impact measurement, though the phrasing of some survey questions makes it difficult to assess this development fully. Thus, a recent survey of impact investors found only 33 percent reporting that they considered "standardized impact metrics" "very important," though another 65 percent were willing to rate them "important" or "somewhat important." Similarly, only 30 percent of responding impact investors reported using "third-party ratings" for "all potential investments," though another 60 percent indicated that they use them "if available." Saltuk et al., *Perspectives on Progress*, 16.

8. Lester M. Salamon, "What Would Google Do? Designing Appropriate Social Impact Measurement Systems," *Community Development Investment Review* 7.2 (December

2011): 43–47. Applied to the field of social-impact measurement, this approach has been termed "constituency voice" and developed formally by David Bonbright through an organization called Keystone. "Constituency Voice," Keystone, accessed February 9, 2013, http://www.keystoneaccountability.org/analysis/constituency.

9. SEEDCO, *The Limits of Social Enterprise* (New York: SEEDCO Policy Center, 2008).

10. E. T. Jackson and Associates, *Accelerating Impact*, xiii.

11. The $8 billion figure comes from a survey of 99 investors identified by the Global Impact Investment Network and J.P. Morgan Social Finance and reporting managing US$10 million or more of impact investment capital as of the end of 2012. The $4.4 billion and $2.5 billion figures come from a similar survey of 52 impact investment intermediaries undertaken by J.P. Morgan in late 2011. See Saltuk et al., *Perspectives on Progress*, 3–4; and Saltuk, Bouri, and Leung, *Impact Investment Market*, 5.

12. "Federal Reserve Statistical Release, Z.l, Flow of Funds Accounts of the United States, March 2011," Board of Governors of the Federal Reserve System, accessed May 11, 2013, http://www.federalreserve.gov.releases/z1/201000311.

13. "Michael Drexler and Abigail Noble, preface to World Economic Forum, *From the Margins to the Mainstream: Assessment of the Impact Investment Sector and Opportunities to Engage Mainstream Investors* (Davos: World Economic Forum, September 2013), 3.

14. Tingerthal, "Securitization," in Salamon, *New Frontiers of Philanthropy*.

15. US SIF Foundation, *Sustainable and Responsible Investing Trends*, 11.

16. Erickson, "Secondary Markets," in Salamon, *New Frontiers of Philanthropy*. For discussions of factors limiting the growth of the social-impact investing industry, see Katie Hill, *Investor Perspectives on Social Enterprise Financing* (London: City of London, Big Lottery Fund, Clearly So, 2011); E. T. Jackson and Associates, *Accelerating Impact*, xiv, 19–20. For J.P. Morgan survey results, see Saltuk, Bouri, and Leung, *Impact Investment Market*, 5. Although continued progress was reported in a 2013 report by J.P. Morgan Social Impact, it was notable that the most the authors could claim was that 58 percent of the respondents to their survey were able to report that "more than a few investors" were "already designing an impact investment strategy" but that only 4 percent of respondents could report that "many investors" were doing so. Saltuk et al., *Perspectives on Progress*, 18.

17. Saltuk, Bouri, and Leung, *Impact Investment Market*, 4. A similar complaint surfaced in second place in a 2013 publication drawing on a similar survey. See Saltuk et al., *Perspectives on Progress*, 9.

18. Venturesome, *Access to Capital: A Briefing Paper* (London: CAF Venturesome, 2011).

19. As E. T. Jackson puts it gingerly in his assessment of the state of the impact-investing industry: "While the impact investing industry has, understandably, been focused largely on its supply side efforts to mobilize and place capital, its leading organizations have done relatively less work on actively developing the capacity of ventures to effectively prepare for capital infusion and to use it effectively." E. T. Jackson and Associates, *Accelerating Impact*, xv.

20. Harvey Koh, Ashish Karamchandani and Robert Katz, *From Blueprint to Scale: The Case for Philanthropy in Impact Investing* (San Francisco: Monitor Group, 2012), 10, accessed February 2, 2013, http://www.mim.monitor.com/downloads/Blueprint_To_Scale/From%20Blueprint%20to%20Scale%20-%20Case%20for%20Philanthropy%20in%20Impact%20Investing_Full%20report.pdf.

21. Koh, Karamchandani, and Katz, *From Blueprint to Scale*, 4–6.

22. Koh, Karamchandani, and Katz, *From Blueprint to Scale*, 15–16.

23. Koh, Karamchandani, and Katz, *From Blueprint to Scale*, 18–19.

24. Starr, "Trouble with Impact Investing"; see also Laura Hattendorf, "The Trouble with Impact Investing: P2," *Stanford Social Innovation Review* 14 (April 18, 2012), 14; Tingerthal, "Securitization."

25. See, for example, Lester M. Salamon, "Of Market Failure, Voluntary Failure, and Third-Party Government: Toward a Theory of Government-Nonprofit Relations in the Modern Welfare State," in Lester M. Salamon, *Partners in Public Service: Government-Nonprofit Relations in the Modern Welfare State* (Baltimore: Johns Hopkins University Press, 1995), 33–52.

Chapter 6

1. Bugg-Levine and Emerson, *Impact Investing*, 90.

2. US SIF Foundation, *Sustainable and Responsible Investing Trends*, 11.

3. US SIF Foundation, *Sustainable and Responsible Investing Trends*, 54; "Highlights of Foundation Yearbook, 2011 Edition," Foundation Center, accessed February 10, 2013, http://foundationcenter.org/gainknowledge/research/pdf/fy2011_highlights.pdf.

4. Usman Hayat, "Do Investment Professionals Know about Impact Investing?" CFA Institute, July 2013, cited in World Economic Forum, *From the Margins to the Mainstream*, 5.

5. World Economic Forum, *From the Margins to the Mainstream*.

6. Bugg-Levine and Emerson, *Impact Investing*, 151.

7. E. T. Jackson and Associates, *Accelerating Impact*, xviii; Frieriech and Fulton, *2009 Monitor Report*, 47–48; Koh, Karamchandani, and Katz, *From Blueprint to Scale*, 7–9.

8. Shirley Sagawa, "A Policy Agenda for the New Frontiers of Philanthropy," Chapter 24 in Salamon, *New Frontiers of Philanthropy*.

9. Frieriech and Fulton, *2009 Monitor Report*, 47; O'Donohoe et al., *Impact Investments*, 76; Ben Thornley, David Wood, Katie Grace, Sarah Sullivan, *Impact Investing: A Framework for Policy Design and Analysis* (n.p.: Insight at Pacific Community Ventures and The Initiative for Responsible Investment at Harvard University, January 2011), 15–16; UN Development Program, *Human Development Report* (New York: UN Development Program, 2011), v.

10. Frieriech and Fulton, *2009 Monitor Report*, 47.

11. E. T. Jackson and Associates, *Accelerating Impact*, 29.

12. E. T. Jackson and Associates, *Accelerating Impact*, 21–27.

13. "About: How It Works," TONIIC, accessed February 24, 2013, http://toniic.com/about/how-it-works/.

14. Frieriech and Fulton, *2009 Monitor Report*, 46.

15. *Encyclical Letter Caritas In Veritate, Of The Supreme Pontiff, Benedict XVI, To the Bishops Priests and Deacons, Men And Women Religious, the Lay Faithful, and All People Of Good Will, On Integral Human Development, In Charity and Truth*, Para. 46, accessed May 5, 2011, http://www.vatican.va/holy_father/benedict_xvi/encyclicals/documents/hf_ben-xvi_enc_20090629_caritas-in-veritate_en.html.

Glossary

Bond. A particularly large type of fixed-income security, usually subjected to a *rating* process by a rating agency to provide assurance to potential investors ("rated bonds"), though unrated bonds, or *notes*, are also used, especially in the social-impact investment universe.

Capital stack. A capital fund that pools different layers, or "tranches," of investment capital, each with its own risk-return characteristics, and therefore each with its own potential class of investors.

Collateral. Any form of asset used as security for a loan to be surrendered to lenders in whole or in part if the loan cannot be repaid.

Community Development Finance Institution. One of a network of approximately 1,300 community development loan funds, venture capital funds, credit unions, and community development banks in the United States that focus on investing in distressed urban and rural communities and have been designated by the US government as eligible to receive support from the federal government's CDFI support fund.

Conversion foundation. A charitable foundation formed out of the process of privatizing some public or quasi-public asset, such as a government-owned enterprise, a government-owned building or other property, specialized streams of revenue under government control (e.g., lotteries), or the conversion of a nonprofit into a for-profit company.

Credit enhancement. A special inducement such as a guarantee added to loans in order to attract lenders into what are perceived as risky investments.

Debt. Any of a number of forms of investment, such as loans, bonds, or mortgages, that convey to investors a claim on repayment of both the original "principal" amount of the investment plus "interest," i.e., a percentage of the original investment, either over time or at an agreed-upon time in the future (the maturity date).

Donor-advised fund. A pool of charitable resources that donors deposit for management in community foundations, corporate-originated charitable funds, or other nonprofit institutions, for which the donors receive the full value of their charitable deduction at the time of deposit and out of which they make charitable contributions to eligible nonprofit organizations over a period of years.

Enterprise broker. An individual or institution that performs the critical middleman function of helping social-purpose investors identify promising ventures capable of meeting their investment objectives.

Equity investment. An investment that gives an investor an ownership share of an enterprise and hence a claim on a portion of any profits the enterprise generates, as well as the opportunity to sell these shares for a profit at a later date.

Finance-first investor. An investor who seeks to achieve a risk-adjusted market rate of return on an investment while still meeting a threshold of social or environmental impact.

Fixed-income security. A huge loan with generally long maturity, typically sold through underwriters or investment banks that market portions of it to various types of investors, including pension funds, insurance companies, and high-net-worth individuals.

Foundation as philanthropic bank. A foundation that makes programmatic use of its assets and not just its grant budget for program-related purposes and that makes extensive use of nongrant forms of assistance to achieve greater leverage with its resources.

Funding collaborative. A network that offers groups of either individual or institutional donors and investors vehicles for collective grant-making or social-purpose investing.

Impact-first investor. An investor who seeks to maximize the social or environmental impact of an investment while still meeting a threshold of financial return.

Investment capital. Revenue that fundamentally goes to build long-term organizational capacity and capabilities through the purchase of such things as equipment, facilities, skills, and strategic planning that are expected to generate annual operating revenue for the organization over the longer haul.

Online portals and exchanges. Organizations that make use of the Internet to facilitate direct provision of cash, commodities, and/or services (paid and volunteer) to recipient social-purpose organizations.

Operating income. The income organizations use to run their ongoing annual operations.

Private equity. An equity investment that is made without the benefit of listing on a registered public exchange.

Program-related Investment (PRI). Support that foundations in the US are permitted to count toward their required minimum distribution, but that they can provide in the form of loans, equity, or other financial instruments to for-profit as well as nonprofit organizations so long as the support does not have a commercial purpose and is in support of the foundation's general charitable mission.

Public equity. An equity investment that is made through a registered public stock exchange.

Quasi-equity. A form of equity investment that allows an investor to benefit from the future revenues of an organization through a royalty payment geared to income rather than a share of any profits earned and that often conveys some advisory role in the management of the organization but not an ownership share.

Rated security. A bond that is rated as creditworthy by one of the quasi-official bond rating agencies, such as Standard and Poor's.

Secondary market. A financial institution that raises capital through the issuance of bonds and uses it to purchase the loans originated by primary lenders, refreshing the capital available to these lenders so they can make additional primary loans.

Secured debt. Debt that is backed by some asset that the lender can seize if a loan is not repaid.

Securitization. A financial process that involves assembling bundles of loans (e.g., mortgage loans) into packages and using them as collateral against which to issue bonds on the capital markets, with the proceeds of the bond sales going to pay for the purchase of the bundles of loans.

Senior debt/loan. A loan or other debt that has a first call on payment or collateral in the event a borrower is unable to pay its debt obligations.

Social stock exchange. A regulated trading platform through which dispersed social-purpose investors can locate and invest in social-purpose enterprises and through which social-purpose enterprises can secure capital they need to expand and grow.

Soft loan. A loan with flexible terms intended to permit start-up firms time to become profitable.

Subordinated debt/loan. A loan or other debt that is paid off only after other lenders or investors are paid, in the event a borrower is unable to pay its full obligations.

Unsecured debt. Debt that is not backed by a particular asset (collateral) that could be seized in the event a loan is not repaid.

Bibliography

Aavishkaar. "About Us." Accessed November 4, 2012. http://www.aavishkaar.in/about-us/.

Aavishkaar. "Investment Approach." Accessed November 4, 2012. http://www.aavishkaar.in/about-us/investment-approach/.

Aavishkaar. "About Us." Accessed August 12, 2012. http://www.aavishkaar.in.

Acumen Fund. "About Us." Accessed August 18, 2012. http://www.acumenfund.org.

Acumen Fund. "About Us." Accessed December 4, 2012. http://www.acumenfund.org/about-us.html.

Acumen Fund. "Acumen Fund Ten Year Report, 2001–2011." Accessed January 2, 2013. http://www.acumenfund.org/uploads/assets/documents/Acumen%20Fund%20Ten%20Year%20Report%202001%20-%202011a_3wcsNw56.pdf.

Angel Investors Network. "About." Accessed October 19, 2012. http://www.angelinvestors.net/about.

Arkansas Capital Corporation Group. "Company History & Information." Accessed May 11, 2013. http://arcapital.com/programs/our-history/.

Bamboo Finance. "The Bamboo Finance Private Equity Group." Accessed May 11, 2013. http://www.bamboofinance.com.

Benjamin, Lean, Julia Sass Rubin, and Sean Zielenbach. "Community Development Financial Institutions: Expanding Access to Capital in Under-served Markets." In *The Community Development Reader*, edited by James DeFilippis and Susan Saegert. New York: Routledge Publications, 2008, 95–105.

Big Society Capital. "How We Are Funded." Accessed May 11, 2013. http://www.bigsocietycapital.com/how-we-are-funded.

Big Society Capital. "Social Investment is a Way of Using Capital to Generate Social Impact as well as Some Financial Return for Investors." Accessed May 11, 2013. http://www.bigsocietycapital.com/what-social-investment.

Bishop, Matthew, and Michael Green. *Philanthrocapitalism: How The Rich Can Save The World*. New York: Bloomsbury Press, 2008.

B-Lab. "About B-lab." Accessed February 5, 2013. http://benefitcorp.net/about-b-lab.

B-Lab. "How GIIRS Works." Accessed February 5, 2013. http://www.giirs.org/about-giirs/how-giirs-works.

Blue Orchard. "Fact Sheet." Accessed May 11, 2013. http://www.blueorchard.com/jahia/webdav/site/blueorchard/shared/Publications%20and%20Resources/BlueOrchard%20Factsheets/0907_Fact%20sheet%202009_EN.pdf.

Board of Governors of the Federal Reserve System. "Federal Reserve Statistical Release, Z.l, Flow of Funds Accounts of the United States, March 2011."Accessed May 11, 2013. http://www.federalreserve.gov.releases/z1/201000311.

Bornstein, David. *How to Change the World: Social Entrepreneurs and the Power of New Ideas*. New York: Oxford University Press, 2004.

Borzaga, Carlos, and Jacques Defourny. *The Emergence of Social Enterprise*. London: Routledge, 2001.

Brown, Lester. *World on the Edge: How to Prevent Environmental and Economic Collapse*. New York: W.W. Norton, 2011. Accessed April 14, 2013. http://www.earth-policy.org/books/wote.

Bugg-Levine, Antony, and Jed Emerson. *Impact Investing: Transforming How We Make Money While Making a Difference*. San Francisco: Jossey-Bass, 2011.

California Wellness Foundation. "Financial Statements." Accessed February 6, 2010. http://www.calwellness.org/assets/docs/annual_report/TCWF_FS_2008.pdf.

Calvert Foundation. "Community Investment Note." Accessed May 11, 2013. http://www.calvertfoundation.org/invest/how-to-invest/community-investment-note.

Calvert Foundation. "Mission and History." Accessed January 2, 2013. http://www.calvertfoundation.org/index.php?option=com_content&view=article&id=66&Itemid=76.

Carmody, Lucy, Benjamin McCarron, Jenny Blinch, and Allison Prevatt. *Impact Investing in Emerging Markets*. Singapore: Responsible Research, 2011.

CEI Ventures. "Overview." Accessed November 3, 2012. http://www.ceiventures.com.

CGAP. "About Us." Accessed October 20, 2012. http://www.cgap.org/p/site/c/aboutus/.

CGAP. "The History of Microfinance." Prepared for CGAP UNCDF donor training, "The New Vision of Microfinance: Financial Services for the Poor." Accessed June 11, 2013. http://www.slideshare.net/JosephSam/the-history-of-microfinance-cgap

Churchill, Craig, and Michael J. McCord. "Emerging Trends in Microinsurance." In *Protecting the Poor: A Microinsurance Compendium*, vol. 2, edited by Craig Churchill and Michal Matul. Geneva: International Labor Organization and Munich Re Foundation, 2012, 8–39.

City of New York, Office of the Mayor. "Mayor Bloomberg, Deputy Mayor Gibbs, and Corrections Commissioner Schriro Announce the Nation's First Social Impact Bond Program." Accessed November 4, 2012. http://www.nyc.gov/html/om/html/2012b/pr285-12.html.

Community Reinvestment Fund. "Quick Facts." Accessed September 1, 2012. http://www.crfusa.com/AboutCRF/Pages/QuickFacts.aspx.

Cooch, Sarah, and Mark Kramer. *Compounding Impact: Mission Investing by U.S. Foundations*. FSG Social Impact Advisors, 2007.

Dighe, Atul. "Demographic and Technological Imperatives." In *The State of Nonprofit America*, 2nd Edition, edited by Lester M. Salamon. Washington, DC: Brookings Institution Press, 2012, 616–638.

Drexler, Michael, and Abigail Noble. Preface to World Economic Forum, *From the Margins to the Mainstream: Assessment of the Impact Investment Sector and*

Opportunities to Engage Mainstream Investors. Davos: World Economic Forum, September 2013. Accessed November 15, 2013. http://www3.weforum.org/docs/WEF_II_FromMarginsMainstream_Report_2013.pdf.

Edna McConnell Clark Foundation. "How We Work." Accessed May 11, 2013. http://www.emcf.org/how-we-work/.

Erickson, David. *The Housing Policy Revolution.* Washington, DC: Urban Institute Press, 2008.

E. T. Jackson and Associates. *Accelerating Impact: Achievements, Challenges and What's Next in Building the Impact Investing Industry.* New York: Rockefeller Foundation, July 2012. Accessed September 14, 2013. http://www.rockefellerfoundation.org/uploads/images/fda23ba9-ab7e-4c83-9218-24fdd79289cc.pdf.

Ethical Property. "How to Invest." Accessed November 4, 2012. http://www.ethical-property.co.uk/howtoinvest.php.

European Venture Philanthropy Association. *European Venture Philanthropy Directory 2010/11.* Brussels: European Venture Philanthropy Association, 2010.

Eurosif. *European SRI Study: 2012.* Brussels: Eurosif, 2012. Accessed May 11, 2013. http://www.eurosif.org/research/eurosif-sri-study/sri-study-2012.

Financial Markets Series. *Bond Markets 2011.* London: TheCityUK, 2011. Accessed May 11, 2013. http://www.thecityuk.com/assets/Uploads/BondMarkets2011.pdf.

Ford Foundation. "About." Accessed February 6, 2010. http://www.fordfound.org/about.

Forum for Sustainable and Responsible Investment. *Report on Sustainable and Responsible Investing Trends in the United States: 2012.* Washington, DC: US SIF, 2012.

Foundation Center. *Foundation Yearbook: Facts and Figures on Private and Community Foundations, 2008 Edition.* New York: Foundation Center, 2008.

Foundation Center. *Foundation Yearbook, 2009.* New York: Foundation Center, 2010.

Foundation Center. "Highlights of Foundation Yearbook, 2011 Edition." Accessed May 10, 2013. http://foundationcenter.org/gainknowledge/research/pdf/fy2011_highlights.pdf.

Freireich, Jessica, and Katherine Fulton. *Investing for Social and Environmental Impact.* San Francisco: Monitor Institute, 2009. Accessed May 11, 2013. http://www.monitorinstitute.com/impactinvesting/documents/InvestingforSocialandEnvImpact_FullReport_004.pdf.

Godeke, Steven, and Raúl Pomares with Albert V. Bruno, Pat Guerra, Charly Kleisner, and Hersh Shefrin. *Solutions for Impact Investors: From Strategy to Implementation.* New York: Rockefeller Philanthropy Advisors, 2009.

Goodall, Emilie, and John Kingston. *Access to Capital: A Briefing Paper.* London: CAF Venturesome, 2009. Accessed February 10, 2013. http://www.marmanie.com/cms/upload/file/CAF_Venturesome_Access_to_Capital_0909.pdf.

Grantmakers in Health. *A Profile of Foundations Created from Health Care Conversions.* Grantmakers in Health, 2009. http://www.gih.org/files/usrdoc/2009_Conversion_Report.pdf.

Grassroots Business Fund. *2011 Annual Report of the Grassroots Business Fund.* Washington, DC: Grassroots Business Fund, 2011. Accessed May 11, 2013. http://gbfund.org/sites/default/files/GBF_AR_2011.pdf.

Habitat for Humanity International. "Flexible Capital Access Program (FlexCap): Investment Summary." Accessed May 11, 2013. https://www.missioninvestors.org/system/files/tools/Habitat%20for%20Humanity%27s%20FlexCAP%20summary.pdf.

Hattendorf, Laura. "The Trouble with Impact Investing: P2." *Stanford Social Innovation Review* Impact Blog, April 18, 2012. Accessed May 13, 2013. http://www.ssireview.org/blog/entry/the_trouble_with_impact_investing_part_2.

Hill, Kate. *Investor Perspectives on Social Enterprise Financing*. London: City of London, Big Lottery Fund, Clearly So, 2011.

HTC Group. "Welcome to HCT Group." Accessed November 4, 2012. http://www.hctgroup.org.

Hub, The. "About." Accessed October 20, 2012. http://www.the-hub.net/about.

Humphreys, Joshua. "Sustainability Trends in US Alternative Investment." US SIF Foundation: Forum for Sustainable and Responsible Investment, 2011. Accessed October 19, 2012. http://www.investorscircle.net/accelsite/media/3195/Sustainability%20Trends%20in%20US%20Alternative%20Investments%20Report.pdf.

Hutton, Robert. "Cameron Opens $1 Billion Big Society Bank to Fund Charities." *Bloomberg*, April 4, 2012. Accessed May 11, 2013. http://www.bloomberg.com/news/2012-04-03/cameron-opens-1-billion-big-society-bank-to-fund-charities.html.

IDB Group. "The IDB Group: Your Partner for Impact Investing in Latin America and the Caribbean." Accessed May 11, 2012. http://idbdocs.iadb.org/wsdocs/getdocument.aspx?docnum=36886146.

IFFIm. "Bonds." Accessed May 11, 2013. http://www.iffim.org/bonds.

Internal Revenue Service. "Notice of Proposed Rulemaking: Examples of Program-Related Investments REG-144267-11." *Internal Revenue Bulletin* 2012–21 (May 21, 2012). Accessed April 13, 2013. http://www.irs.gov/irb/2012-21_IRB/ar11.html.

International Association of Microfinance Investors. "Microfinance Investment." Accessed May 11, 2013. http://www.iamfi.com/microfinance_investment.html.

International Labour Organization. "Microinsurance Innovation Facility." Accessed May 11, 2013. www.ilo.org/microinsurance.

Jolly, David, and Jack Ewing. "Unemployment in Euro Zone Reaches New High." *New York Times*, November 30, 2012. Accessed May 11, 2013. http://www.nytimes.com/2012/12/01/business/global/daily-euro-zone-watch.html.

Kansas Venture Capital. "Kansas Venture Capital, Inc. ('KVCI')." Accessed May 11, 2013. http://www.kvci.com/.

Kentucky Highlands Investment Corporation. "Equity Investments." Accessed November 3, 2012. http://www.khic.org/equity.html.

Keystone Accountability. "Constituency Voice." Accessed February 9, 2013. http://www.keystoneaccountability.org/analysis/constituency.

Kiva. "About." Accessed October 20, 2012. http://www.kiva.org/about/stats.

Koh, Harvey, Ashish Karamchandani, and Robert Katz. *From Blueprint to Scale: The Case for Philanthropy in Impact Investing*. San Francisco: Monitor Group, 2012.

Lawrence, Steven. "Doing Good with Foundation Assets: An Updated Look at Program-Related Investments." In *The PRI Directory*, 3rd ed, edited by Foundation Center. New York: Foundation Center, 2010, xiii–xx.

Lawrence, Steven, and Reina Mukai. *Key Facts on Mission Investing*. New York: Foundation Center, 2011.

Letts, Christine, William Ryan, and Allen Grossman. "Virtuous Capital: What Foundations can Learn from Venture Capitalists." *Harvard Business Review* (March–April 1997): 36–46.

Living Cities. "History." Accessed October 19, 2012. http://www.livingcities.org/about/history/.

Markets for Good. *Markets for Good: Upgrading the Information Infrastructure for Social Change*. 2012. Accessed May 11, 2013. http://www.marketsforgood.org/wordpress/wp-content/uploads/2012/11/MarketsforGood_Information-Infrastructure_Fall-2012_.pdf.

Massachusetts Capital Resource Company. "Mass Capital, Company." Accessed May 11, 2013. http://www.masscapital.com/company/.

McKinsey and Company. *And the Winner is… Capturing the Promise of Philanthropic Prizes*. 2009. Accessed May 13, 2013. http://mckinseyonsociety.com/downloads/reports/Social-Innovation/And_the_winner_is.pdf.

Microfinance Africa. "USAID and Impact Investors Capitalize New Equity Fund for East African Agribusiness." Accessed May 11, 2013. http://seedstock.com/2011/10/05/usaid-global-impact-investing-network-join-to-create-east-africa-agricultural-investment-fund/.

Mission Investors Exchange. "About Mission Investors Exchange." Accessed October 20, 2012. http://www.missioninvestors.org/about-us/origins-mission-investors-exchange.

Mission Investors Exchange. "The Origins of Mission Investors Exchange." Accessed October 20, 2012. http://www.missioninvestors.org/about-us/origins-mission-investors-exchange.

Mission Investors Exchange. "What's New in Mission Investing?" Accessed October 20, 2012. https://www.missioninvestors.org/whats-new.

Monitor Institute. "Investing for Social & Environmental Impact: A Design for Catalyzing an Emerging Industry." Accessed May 11, 2013. http://www.monitorinstitute.com/impactinvesting/documents/InvestingforSocialandEnvImpact_FullReport_004.pdf.

National Philanthropic Trust. "2011 Donor-Advised Fund Report." Accessed May 11, 2013. http://www.nptrust.org/images/uploads/2011%20Donor-Advised-Fund-Report%281%29.pdf.

NESTA. "About Us." Accessed May 11, 2013. http://www.nesta.org.uk/.

Net Impact. "Home Page." Accessed October 1, 2012. http://netimpact.org/.

New Energy Finance. "Global Trends in Clean Energy Investment: Q4 2009 Clean Energy Fact Pack." Accessed May 11, 2013. http://about.bnef.com/fact-packs/global-trends-in-clean-energy-investment-q4-2009-fact-pack/.

New Profit. "About Us." Accessed May 11, 2013. http://newprofit.com/cgi-bin/iowa/about/9.html.

Nichols, Alex. *Social Entrepreneurship: New Models of Sustainable Social Change.* Oxford: Oxford University Press, 2006.

O'Donohoe, Nick, Christina Leijonhufvud, Yasemin Saltuk, Antongy Bugg-Levine, and Margot Brandenburg. *Impact Investments: An Emerging Asset Class.* New York: J.P. Morgan, 2010.

Opportunity Finance Network. "CDFI Data Project." Accessed May 11, 2013. http://www.opportunityfinance.net/industry/default.aspx?id=236.

Opportunity Finance Network. "About." Accessed October 12, 2012. http://www.opportunityfinance.net/about.

Prahalad, C. K. *The Fortune at the Bottom of the Pyramid: Eradicating Poverty through Profits.* Philadelphia: Wharton School Publishing, 2004.

Popper, Nathan. "Even with Fiscal Agreement, Investors Facing Imminent Obstacles." *New York Times*, January 1, 2013. Accessed September 14, 2013. http://www.nytimes.com/2013/01/02/business/economy/daily-stock-market-activity.html?_r=0.

Reed, Stanley, and Mark Scott. "In Europe, Paid Permits for Pollution Are Fizzling." *New York Times*, April 22, 2013.

Roth, Jim, Denis Garand, and Stuart Rutherford. *The Landscape of Microinsurance in the World's 100 Poorest Countries.* Appleton, WI: Microinsurance Center, 2007.

Rural Housing and Economic Development Gateway, US Department of Housing and Urban Development. "Kentucky Highlands Investment Corporation." Accessed March 2, 2013. http://www.hud.gov/offices/cpd/economicdevelopment/programs/rhed/gateway/pdf/KentuckyHighlands.pdf.

Salamon, Lester M. *America's Nonprofit Sector: A Primer.* 3rd ed. New York: Foundation Center, 2012.

Salamon, Lester M., editor. *New Frontiers of Philanthropy: A Guide to the New Tools and Actors Reshaping Global Philanthropy and Social Investing.* New York: Oxford University Press, 2014.

Salamon, Lester M. "Of Market Failure, Voluntary Failure, and Third-Party Government: Toward a Theory of Government-Nonprofit Relations in the Modern Welfare State." In Lester M. Salamon, *Partners in Public Service: Government-Nonprofit Relations in the Modern Welfare State.* Baltimore: Johns Hopkins University Press, 1995, 33–52.

Salamon, Lester M. *Philanthropication thru Privatization: Building Assets for Social Progress.* New York: East-West Management Institute, 2013. http://bit.ly/1brWDcL.

Salamon, Lester M. "Privatization for the Social Good: A New Avenue for Global Foundation-Building." In *The PB Report: 2009*, edited by The Privatization Barometer. July 2010.

Salamon, Lester M. *Rethinking Corporate Social Engagement: Lessons from Latin America.* Sterling, VA: Kumarian Press, 2010.

Salamon, Lester M. "The Rise of the Nonprofit Sector." *Foreign Affairs* 73.4 (July–August 1994): 109–22.

Salamon, Lester M., editor. *The State of Nonprofit America.* 2nd ed. Washington, DC: Brookings Institution Press, 2012.

Salamon, Lester M. *The Tools of Government: A Guide to the New Governance.* New York: Oxford University Press, 2002.

Salamon, Lester M. "What Would Google Do? Designing Appropriate Social Impact Measurement Systems." *Community Development Investment Review* 7.2 (December 2011): 43–47.

Salamon, Lester M., and Stephanie Geller. "Investment Capital: The New Challenge for American Nonprofits." Johns Hopkins Nonprofit Listening Post Project (2006). Accessed May 11, 2013. http://ccss.jhu.edu/publications-findings?did=265.

Saltuk, Yasemin, Amit Bouri, and Giselle Leung. *Insight into the Impact Investment Market: An In-Depth Analysis of Investor Perspectives and over 2,200 Transactions.* London: J.P. Morgan Social Finance Research, 2011. Accessed November 16, 2013. http://www.thegiin.org/cgi-bin/iowa/download?row=334&field=gated_download_1.

Saltuk, Yasemin, Amit Bouri, Abhilash Mudaliar, and Min Pease. *Perspectives on Progress: The Impact Investor Survey.* London: J.P. Morgan Global Social Finance, 2013. Accessed April 14, 2013. http://www.jpmorganchase.com/corporate/socialfinance/document/207350_JPM_Perspectives_on_Progress_2013-01-07_1018749_ada.pdf.

Schwartz, Rob. *Social Investment.* London: Clearly So, 2012.

SEEDCO. *The Limits of Social Enterprise.* New York: SEEDCO Policy Center, 2008.

SeedStock. "USAID, Global Impact Investing Network Join to Create East Africa Agricultural Investment Fund." Accessed May 11, 2013. http://seedstock.com/2011/10/05/usaid-global-impact-investing-network-join-to-create-east-africa-agricultural-investment-fund/.

Small Enterprise Assistance Fund (SEAF). "Our Impact." Accessed June 6, 2013. http://seaf.com/index.php?option=com_content&view=article&id=36&Itemid=82&lang=en.

Social Enterprise UK. *Fightback Britain: A Report on the State of Social Enterprise Survey 2011.* London: Social Enterprise UK, 2011

Social Finance. "Home." Accessed November 4, 2012. http://www.socialfinance.uk/print9.T

Social Finance. *A New Tool for Scaling Impact: How Social Impact Bonds Can Mobilize Private Capital to Advance Social Good.* Boston: Social Finance, 2012. Accessed November 4, 2012. http://www.socialfinance.org.uk/resources/social-finance/new-tool-scaling-impact-how-social-impact-bonds-can-mobilize-private-capita.

Social Investment Forum. "About Us." Accessed October 20, 2012. http://www.socialinvest.org.

Starr, Kevin. "The Trouble with Impact Investing: P1." *Stanford Social Investment Review* (January 24, 2012). Accessed May 11, 2013. http://www.ssireview.org/blog/entry/the_trouble_with_impact_investing_part_1.

Stein, Peer, Tony Goland, and Robert Schiff. *Two Trillion and Counting: Assessing the Credit Gap for Micro, Small, and Medium-Size Enterprises in the Developing World.* Washington, DC: International Finance Corporation and McKinsey & Company, 2010.

Strauss, William, and Neil Howe. *Millennials Rising: The Next Great Generation.* New York: Vantage, 2000.

Swiss Reinsurance Company. *Microinsurance—Risk Protection for 4 Billion People.* Zurich: Swiss Re, 2010.

TechSoupGlobal. "TechSoup Global by the Numbers, Quarterly Report, October 2010." Accessed May 11, 2013. http://www.techsoupglobal.org/press/selectcoverage.

Thomas, Landon, Jr. "As the Bailouts Continue in Europe, So Does the Flouting of Rules." *New York Times*, November 29, 2012.

Thornley, Ben, and Colby Dailey. "Building Scale in Community Impact Investing Through Nonfinancial Performance Measurement." *Community Development Investment Review* 6.1 (2010). Accessed May 13, 2013. http://www.frbsf.org/community-development/files/Thornley_Dailey.pdf.

Thornley, Ben, David Wood, Katie Grace, and Sarah Sullivan, *Impact Investing: A Framework for Policy Design and Analysis*. N.P.: Insight at Pacific Community Ventures and The Initiative for Responsible Investment at Harvard University, January 2011.

TONIIC. "Global Gathering." Accessed October 19, 2012. http://toniicglobalgathering.eventbrite.com/.

TONIIC. "About: How It Works." Accessed February 24, 2013. http://toniic.com/about/how-it-works/.

Tzetzes, John. *Book of Histories (Chiliades)*. Translated by Francis R. Walton. N.P.: Lipsiae, 1826.

United Nations Development Program. *Human Development Report*. New York: United Nations Development Program, 2011.

United Nations Principles for Responsible Investment. "About Us." Accessed October 20, 2012. http://www.unpri.org.

United States Census Bureau. *Statistical Abstract of the United States, 2012*. Accessed May 10, 2013. http://www.census.gov/compendia/statab/cats/banking_finance_insurance/financial_assets_and_liabilities.html.

United States Social Investment Forum Foundation. *Report on Sustainable and Responsible Investing Trends in the United States: 2012*. Washington, DC: US SIF, 2012.

Vatican, The. *Encyclical Letter Caritas In Veritate, Of The Supreme Pontiff, Benedict XVI, To the Bishops Priests and Deacons, Men And Women Religious, the Lay Faithful, and All People Of Good Will, On Integral Human Development, In Charity and Truth*. Accessed May 5, 2011. http://www.vatican.va/holy_father/benedict_xvi/encyclicals/documents/hf_ben-xvi_enc_20090629_caritas-in-veritate_en.html.

Velasquez, Christa. "Advancing Social Impact Investment Through Measurement." Comments at Federal Reserve. Accessed May 11, 2013. http://www.frbsf.org/cdinvestments/conferences/social-impact-investments/transcript/Velasquez_Panel_3.pdf.

Venturesome. *Access to Capital: A Briefing Paper*. London: CAF Venturesome, 2011.

Vogel, David. *The Market for Virtue: The Potential and Limits of Corporate Social Responsibility*. Washington, DC: Brookings Institution Press, 2005.

Volunteer Match. "Our 2011 Annual Report Infographic." Accessed October 23, 2012. http://blogs.volunteermatch.org/engagingvolunteers/2012/06/25/our-2011-annual-report-infographic-the-story-of-you/.

Weaver, Evan. "Marrying Cash and Change: Social 'Stock Markets' Spread Worldwide." *Christian Science Monitor*, August 30, 2012. Accessed March 3, 2012. http://

www.csmonitor.com/World/Making-a-difference/Change-Agent/2012/0830/ Marrying-cash-and-change-Social-stock-markets-spread-worldwide.

Willow Impact Investors. "Investment Policy." Accessed March 2, 2013. http:// www.willowimpact.com/about-us/company/investment-policy.html.

Willow Impact Investors. "About Us: Our Team." Accessed August 10, 2012. http:// www.willowimpact.com/about-us/.

World Bank. *State and Trends of the Carbon Market*. Washington, DC: World Bank Group, 2011. Accessed May 11, 2013. http://siteresources.worldbank.org/ intcarbonfinance/Resources.

World Economic Forum. *From the Margins to the Mainstream*. Davos: World Economic Forum, September 2013. http://www3.weforum.org/docs/WEF_ II_FromMarginsMainstream_Report_2013.pdf.

Young, Dennis R., Lester M. Salamon, and Mary Clark Grinsfelder. "Commercialization, Social Ventures, and For-Profit Competition." In *The State of Nonprofit America*, edited by Lester M. Salamon. Washington, DC: Brookings Institution Press, 2012, 521–548.

About the Author

Lester M. Salamon is a Professor at The Johns Hopkins University and Director of the Johns Hopkins Center for Civil Society Studies. He previously served as the founding director of the Johns Hopkins Institute for Policy Studies, as the director for Governance and Management Research at the Urban Institute in Washington, D.C., and as deputy associate director of the U.S. Office of Management and Budget. Dr. Salamon is an expert on the tools of government and has been a pioneer in the empirical study of the non-profit sector in the United States and around the world. His book, *America's Nonprofit Sector: A Primer*, is the standard text used in college-level courses on the nonprofit sector in the United States. His *Partners in Public Service: Government and the Nonprofit Sector in the Modern Welfare State* won the 1996 ARNOVA Award for Distinguished Book in Nonprofit and Voluntary Action Research, and in 2012 was awarded the Aaron Wildavsky Enduring Contribution Award from the American Political Science Association. Dr. Salamon's recent books include *The Tools of Government: A Guide to the New Governance* (Oxford University Press, 2002); *Global Civil Society: Dimensions of the Nonprofit Sector* (Kumarian Press, 2004); *Rethinking Corporate Social Responsibility: Lessons from Latin America* (Kumarian Press, 2010); *America's Nonprofit Sector: A Primer*, Third Edition (Foundation Center, 2012); and *The State of Nonprofit America*, Second Edition. (Brookings Institution Press, 2012). Dr. Salamon received his B.A. degree in Economics and Policy Studies from Princeton University and his Ph.D. in Government from Harvard University. He served from 1998 to 2006 as the Chairman of the Board of the Chesapeake Community Foundation.

Index